Praise for Dr. Pat

"Most doctors get into medicine to serve the greater good and help us all live better, stronger and longer lives, which then negatively impacts their own health and family life. In *Burn-In*, Patrick Tran shows how to make the world of medicine a balanced place—a win-win. This book proves that a doctor can indeed have it all."

—Pat Hiban *New York Times* bestselling author of *6 Steps to 7 Figures* and *Tribe of Millionaires*, cofounder of GoBundance

"I have been fortunate to witness the incredible growth in wisdom and life perspective Dr. Tran has developed while dealing with his young son's surprise illness. I've seen him gain a depth of understanding of what is important in life that few of us reach. His ability to articulate this new mindset to help others is more than impressive. I know I am a better person because of the wisdom of Dr. Patrick Tran."

—Darryl Putnam, speaker, writer, investor and entrepreneur

"Dr. Patrick Tran has changed my life by teaching me meditation and mindset through his calming presence. He navigates medicine effortlessly while being fully present for his son's journey surviving cancer. Despite overwhelming odds, he has crushed it in business, completing over $20,000,000 in triple net real estate transactions with me in less than 12 months, which we plan to more than double every year. If you want fulfillment in your life while having both time and financial freedom, Patrick can show you the way!"

—Matt Onofrio DNAP, CRNA, CEO Wild Moose Ventures

"Dr. Tran is a kind-hearted, genuine soul who is on a mission to improve the lives of physicians by teaching them the path to financial freedom through real estate investing. He is a truly great person who brings together robust real estate experience and solid values."

—Elaine Stageberg MD, psychiatrist, founder of Black Swan Investing and founder of Single Family Investing at Scale

"Patrick Tran is an inspiration to be around. Both a constant humble learner and incredibly insightful, he brings a depth of knowledge that is rare in today's quick sound bite era. His action-oriented life is impressive and makes you want to be around him. I recommend anyone given the chance to spend time with Patrick in whatever capacity you can."

—Jake Harris, bestselling author of *Catching Knives: A Guide to Investing in Distressed Commercial Real Estate*, managing partner at Harris Bay

"Dr. Patrick Tran lives the gratitude and positivity he teaches and is wise beyond his years. His energy is desperately needed to revive the devalued physician in our disrupted medical profession."

—Brett Levine MD, head and neck surgeon and coauthor of *How to Join, Buy, or Merge a Physician's Practice*

"I have witnessed Patrick's son's cancer journey through his writings. As a cancer survivor, I can relate to what he's gone through. He is evolving and growing in his deep wisdom about life and I am thankful for every word he writes, as it helps me to reflect more and surrender to what is in the moment."

—Nina Homnack, cofounder and SVP of SimulTrans

"Patrick Tran is a sincere and caring person who will be there to listen to your needs."

—Wilson Leung, founder of OWN Real Estate

"Patrick Tran has the knowledge and skills to help doctors build their financial freedom. It is much needed in the medical industry today."

—Tim Rhode, founder of 1Life Fully Lived 501c3, author of *1Life RoadMap Journal* and *Tribe of Millionaires*

"Dr. Patrick Tran is insightful and wise beyond his years. He has an uncanny ability to identify the source of burnout amongst physicians and present a way out. His program of action and the tools he uses to create fulfillment in the here and now is cold water in a parched land. If you're stuck and looking for more, act now! And go with Patrick! You'll be glad you did."

—Dr. Joe Martin DNP, CRNA, president of Advanced Anesthesia Inc.

"Dr. Tran is an outstanding individual who cares deeply about those around him. He strives to help others unlock their potential through compassion, empathy and positivity and empowers others to embrace a mindset revolving around wholesome happiness. I highly recommend working with him."

—Hersh Rai, Managing Partner, RaiVu Capital

"When I first talked with Dr. Tran, I could immediately recognize his genuine compassion for others, drive to get things done and extensive knowledge in real estate. His energy and positive mindset is contagious. I look forward to continue working with Dr. Tran and I recommend everyone find an excuse to get in touch with him."

—Nicholas Vu, managing partner of RaiVu Capital

"Happiness is an attitude, rather than a destination. In *Burn-In*, Patrick Tran teaches us that, with the right attitude, we can overcome obstacles and achieve greatness. This book can help improve the lives of a generation of doctors, and that will benefit us all."

—Tom Burns MD, orthopedic surgeon, principal and cofounder of Presario Ventures and bestselling author of *Why Doctors Don't Get Rich*

"Dr. Patrick Tran is truly heart-centered in everything he does. You can't help but feel that he is naturally 'here' permanently —a true hallmark of anti-stress, anti-anxiety and anti-burnout. He's been able to shift the direction of his life by tapping into his inner abundance and patience and it clearly shows in his book and interactions with others."

—Derek Clifford, author of *Part-Time Real Estate Investing for Full-Time Professionals: Upgrade Your Mindset, Portfolio and Finances in Less Than a Year While Working*

"Burnout is a significant problem in medicine. Many feel it is inevitable and even their fault, but Dr. Patrick Tran is a thought leader and results leader who shows us a different path. Dr. Tran's insights and actionable tools are life and career changing! This book should be required reading for medical students. I believe it could change the future of how we practice medicine."

—Jaime Hope MD, emergency room physician and best-selling author of *Habit That!*

BURN-IN

A Doctor's Guide to Finding Happiness,
Avoiding Burnout and Catching FIRE
(Financial Independence, Retire Early)

Dr. Patrick Tran

LEGACY
launch pad
PUBLISHING

ISBN: 978-1-951407-93-3 (ebook)

ISBN: 978-1-951407-95-7 (paperback)

ISBN: 978-1-951407-96-4 (hardcover)

To physicians everywhere: recall that in the Hippocratic oath, one of the first lines is "Primum non nocere," which means "First, do no harm."

Remember this applies to you also! Take care of yourself first so that you can better serve others. On a plane, they tell you to put on your own oxygen mask so you don't pass out before you can help your child or the person next to you. Don't take the hypocritical oath, in which you disregard yourself and burn out by giving all of your precious energy away.

Turn your attention inward so that you can lead a life of infinite joy and draw from a deep well of compassion to care for not only yourself but also your family, your patients, the entire world and beyond.

Contents

Foreword

During the 13 years I spent as a student after graduating from high school—from medical school through residency and fellowship—I learned nothing about money. The whole medical training system encourages significant memorization of complex subjects like biochemistry, genetics and physiology. But on the subject of how to make a life—a happy life—as a working doctor, the instructions are scant if not entirely absent.

There is a chasmic gap in financial education and literacy in medical training and beyond. In fact, money—for doctors, nurses and other people who choose medical professions—can be a taboo subject. You're supposed to pursue a medical career because it is a calling, a profession, a noble service. Where does money fit into this? Many of our fellow teammates—doctors, dentists, CRNAs, nurses, pharmacists, dietitians, you-name-it therapists (physical, speech, occupational)—still don't know after decades into their careers. Which of your professors or attending physicians ever discussed their net worth or salary with you? How many of your peers talked openly about student loan debt or about the parental or spousal support that allowed them to pursue opportunities without considering the expense?

As a resident physician, you're working 80-hour weeks and being paid somewhere around $50,000 per year. You have no sense of control. You're scheduled for this 16-hour shift or that overnight shift or 30-hour shift. They say jump and you're expected to ask, "How high?"

When you're done with training, you're a full-fledged attending physician and you get your first job. Maybe you're a W2 employee. Your hours might not be as bad as they were in residency: yes, you may be paid significantly more, but you're not a stereotypical rich doctor, are you? After all the sacrifice of your 20s and 30s spent in education, you come out on the other side hundreds of thousands of dollars in debt.

As an attending, the stakes are a bit higher. It's your license, reputation and malpractice insurance on the line if you make a mistake. In our litigious society, you may worry that your patients will hit you with a frivolous (or not-so-frivolous) lawsuit. Maybe you rub someone the wrong way, and they write a nasty review about you on Yelp that causes new appointments to drop off.

If you're employed, you might be treated like a commodity by the guys running the show. I am a board-certified dermatologist, and there are many conflicts in my field. Private equity (PE) groups have been rolling up dermatology practices, buying them, making them more efficient and selling them at a profit. This has been great for some older dermatologists exiting their practices and capitalizing on their years of service to their patients. There have also been very public failures by PE groups such as U.S. Dermatology Partners defaulting on a $377 *million* dollar loan.

The PE groups aren't going anywhere—they have been and will always be a part of medicine now. Medicine is a calling to you as a doctor, but it is a business at the end of the day, and there are many ways to divide the pie. While health-care costs have risen exponentially, the salaries of doctors have not. The money's not going to you, and at times, doctors are unfairly scapegoated for their seemingly high salaries.

You spend all day caring for patients, trying to express empathy, treating illness and helping others. But it may wear on you. You may end the workday tired and exhausted, with nothing left to give. What about when you get home? Now it's time to put on a show and be a great life partner, spouse and active parent. Do you live in a nice home like doctors are supposed to? Do you drive a nice car like doctors are supposed to? Are you always trying to keep up with the Joneses?

And this, I should say, is often the best-case scenario. For nurses, EMTs and other people who work closely with doctors and in hospital and clinic settings, the same pressures often apply even though salaries are lower.

This is where burnout comes from. It arises from a loss of control over your life. The constant give, give, give to the patients in your day job can drain even the most compassionate person. The grind of the non-productive administrative burden of clicking boxes to produce long, useless blocks of text, smart phrases and "vital" information on electronic medical records is soul-sucking. With the move away from paper charts and a shift to mindless computer transcriptions on electronic medical records (EMR), the signal gets lost in a sea of noise. Tell me I'm wrong—that you've never read an EMR note with copy-pasted material from the day before that was never updated. One of the worst ones I've seen had the physical exam part of the note stating "patient remains intubated and sedated" when in fact, the plan the day before had been to extubate—and the patient was now awake, alert and speaking!

Burnout is a feeling of not having enough money, time or both to do what you love with those you love. It is the question, "What did I do all of this for?" These are giant, waving red flags in your life screaming, "Go back! This is not the way!" In the words of Gandalf, these feelings of burnout are a magical staff crashing down, shouting, "You shall not pass!"

But there is a way to avoid burnout. I've been through the same pains as you (and trust me, I know about pain). What I've come to believe is that there is always a way back. A better path leading to better health, better wealth, better quality time and infinite joy. My hope is that you walk it with me and never feel that sense of hopelessness and victimhood again.

I wrote this book as a little treasure map for those seeking a life of true happiness and liberation. I've brought you tools that have helped me in my life so that you can apply them to yours and hit your targets and key performance indicators (KPIs) to become financially independent faster than you think—all while being joyful and grateful along the way.

This book will introduce you to useful tools that will help you find your way back to joy. You will consider what it means to experience an elevated mindset to increase your productivity in life, fight procrastination and live at a higher frequency of vibration, one where your heart and mind are open and aligned with the ultimate version of yourself.

You will learn how to convert your day job or W2 income into passive income so you don't have to work that day job unless you want to. You can carve out the life you desire from the raw block of marble you've been given. If you're just starting out or just considering a career in medicine, I hope you'll find advice in this book on what to do and what not to do. If you've been working as a doctor or a nurse or any other allied health professional for years, I hope you'll find empathy for what you've gone through and support on how to envision a brighter future.

I also want to spell out some commonsense things because people can have unrealistic expectations in life, so let me be totally upfront with you about what exactly you are holding in your hands. This book is not a comprehensive autobiography because I'm not Warren Buffett and I don't want to bore you with 960 pages. This is not a textbook on real estate, business, stocks, bonds, fixed income securities or cryptocurrency investing. This is not a get-rich-quick scheme. I think of this book more like an illustration of the Promised Land, but you are the one who must journey through the desert. I'm not saying it will take you 40 years though—I'd rather you take helicopter flying lessons and get there in a day! The book is only 163 pages—it's not the entirety of the internet nor is it Google, so don't expect it to be. Just relax, enjoy and get whatever nuggets you like—maybe re-read it if you missed something the first time.

I'm also going to give you a TLDR for the book. For those of you whose dopamine receptors cannot get their fix fast enough, here are three nuggets I'll give you as an amuse-bouche:

1. Keep a Beginner's Mind
2. Be Kind
3. Think Critically for Yourself

If you want to find out more about what these mean, I'll give you an afterword with fleshed-out paragraphs when you're done with the book. Or just skip ahead—it's your book now. It's a free country (if you're reading this, for example, in America). Write in it, read it, don't read it, let it collect dust on your shelf, burn it, whatever—I just hope that you enjoy it in some form or fashion.

Finally, remember that this book is just the beginning. Once you have peeked over the wall, you will want to live on the other side. There is a tribe of like-minded individuals, a community of doctors who live by these principles. You can find us at wealthbound.com. Here, these ideas will be iterated, refined and expanded as our network of high-level individuals synergizes and organizes to form its own higher-level organism. We are all jumping in the river of life in a big way, and together we rise the tide and lift each other up. Come join us and see how you can transform your life for the better.

Introduction

Fourteen centimeters.

In the grand scheme of things, it's an incredibly small measurement—the size of a pencil maybe, or the palm of your hand.

But in the doctor's office, on images of the inside of my son's body? Fourteen centimeters felt like it might as well have been a hundred miles. There on the glowing X-ray, pushing so hard it was displacing his small organs, it was all I could see.

How did this happen? How did I end up here? My almost two-year-old son Adrian was sick with an incredibly rare form of cancer, and my wife and I were suddenly facing the prospect of losing our precious boy before he even started kindergarten. I'm a physician, but Adrian's illness was way outside my specialty, which put me in a difficult position: I knew enough to understand how serious the situation was, but I didn't know how to fix it. A father's (and doctor's) worst nightmare. I stayed up all night reading whatever I could find, hoping more knowledge might somehow make the situation easier to digest.

My wife was the first person to see that something was wrong. Adrian, she noticed, only seemed to be gaining weight in one part of his abdomen. Still, while it seemed like he might have been a little smaller than before, he was an otherwise healthy kid—no fevers, no pain, no indication that he was anything other than a happily growing little boy.

But giving him a bath one night, the fact that one side of his small stomach was bigger than the other was unmistakable to her. The diagnosis wasn't instant, but when it came, things started moving at lightning speed. Within two weeks, he would have surgery to remove the tumor, officially called a clear cell sarcoma of the kidney (CCSK). Immediately there was a complication: something called an intussusception, which required the surgeons to go back into his small belly and stop his bowels from telescoping into each other. Once the surgical part of the treatment was complete, we moved on to radiation and over six months of chemotherapy—a process that would be hard on the body of a healthy, full-grown adult, let alone a boy still small enough to be carried in my arms.

It should go without saying that neither my wife nor I got much sleep in the months after Adrian's diagnosis. Our lives were turned upside down with whole days and weeks revolving around doctor's appointments and making sure Adrian was as safe as possible at home.

Whereas most kids his age delight in their newfound mobility, crashing into walls and sliding down playground equipment at the park, Adrian suddenly seemed so fragile— the slightest accident could mean an internal bleed that would seep into his belly, his joints, even his brain. A cold that would usually mean nothing more than a few snuggly days in front of *Cocomelon* could mean rushing Adrian to the hospital where he would need to have blood cultures taken, lab work drawn, broad spectrum antibiotics infused through his central port access, possibly multiple transfusions of blood or platelets and a hospital admission that could last anywhere from two days to two weeks.

And in the moments when Adrian was asleep, exhausted from the seemingly endless treatments, we worried. Would he make it to his next birthday? Would he go to school, make friends, become a person with wants and needs and hopes and dreams? Would we, his parents, be strong enough to see him through this? And if the worst happened, and Adrian died before we did—would we be strong enough to survive that?

———

Adrian's cancer isn't just rare—it's *incredibly* rare. According to Dr. Elizabeth Mullen, a pediatric hematologist/oncologist at the Dana Farber Cancer Institute at Harvard:

> I think it is important to understand that all pediatric cancer is rare, and that CCSK is a very rare subtype of pediatric kidney cancer. To give you some better understanding of how often this type of cancer is seen, over the last 14 years, the Children's Oncology Group (COG) has run a large collaborative renal tumor biology and risk stratification study that opened in 2006 (COG Protocol AREN03B2).
>
> There are 209 sites within the United States and Canada that enroll patients in this study (that is the vast majority of sites that treat children with cancer in those locations) and the study has now enrolled over 6000 children with pediatric renal tumors. There are about 500 new renal tumors in children that occur each year. The vast majority of the tumors seen are Wilms tumor.

The total enrollment of children with Clear Cell Sarcoma of the Kidney since 2006 is just under 200 children, about 14 children a year. This helps to explain why it is necessary to study children with this disease in large collaborative groups of institutions in order to understand how to best treat this disease.

Fourteen children per year in all the United States and Canada! Keep in mind that the population of children under age five in both countries combined is about 24 million. The chance of a child getting this cancer is less than one in a million. And Adrian is one of them. It's almost as rare as winning the lottery, except this isn't a lottery anyone would want to win.

And yet.

Adrian's diagnosis awakened something in me. I've spent my whole life focused on becoming a doctor, on being a doctor and on being a *successful* doctor. Within the span of a few short years, my whole life changed. I had a wife and a family who loved me and needed me. I had a son whose future was, in so many ways, painfully uncertain. It wasn't something I recognized instantly, but over time, I came to see that while I was on this journey with my son and my wife, I was also on another journey that would push me to reconsider so much of what I believed about life and so much about what was out there for me.

Last year, I thought that science, Western medicine and biology were all there was. I was a very logical guy, and I wouldn't believe anything until I saw it with my own two eyes or there was a randomized, placebo-controlled, double-blinded study to prove it. Meditation? Prayer? Law of attraction? Despite growing up in Northern California, which is often thought of as ground zero for everything that falls under the "woo-woo" umbrella, I'd never had much interest in anything that couldn't be proven as factually, scientifically, unequivocally correct.

But little by little (and then all at once), my mind started to open to other possibilities. To the possibility that my son's illness wasn't just a curse but also a gift, one that would allow me to practice and choose radical acceptance, radical love and radical happiness for myself, even on the worst days—especially on the worst days. What if I allowed life to unfold as it was meant to, with me as a humble recipient of everything the world had to offer? What if I learned to turn the love I felt for my son inward, to give love to myself, and then turned it outward again, extending it to other people, too?

I also started to think about how changing my mindset would change my work life. So much of becoming a doctor is about delayed gratification: skipping parties to study in college, forgoing relationships to focus on medical school, dealing with overwork and underpayment in residency, all in the hopes of someday pulling down the high salaries and social prestige that draw so many people to the profession in the first place.

So, what actually happens when you make it (or *if* you make it)? Are doctors happy? Evidence would suggest we're not: over the last year and a half, the news is filled with stories about doctors who overworked themselves during the pandemic, in some cases to the point of severe depression and even suicide. And how many doctors—supposedly one of the most stable and secure professions in the country—lost their jobs?

Even in normal times, burnout is a fact of life for many in the medical field: Medscape's 2017 Lifestyle survey reported that 51 percent of surveyed doctors described themselves as burned out. And it's funny: for every patient who reports feeling dissatisfied (or worse) with the medical system in the United States, there's a doctor who feels the same way, largely for the same reasons. That same 2017 study counted "too much time spent performing bureaucratic tasks," "spending too many hours at work" and "feeling like a cog in a wheel" as reasons cited by doctors for their unhappiness.

What I want to do is offer a solution to burnout. I want to teach my fellow doctors to *burn-in*.

I want you to consider: even the word *burnout* has the word *out* in it! It puts the blame on the *out*side when truly, the onus is on you to create joy and cultivate peace, calm and love *in*side. It's as if in burnout there are all these external factors that both create and solve your problems: a hospital or medical school will get you a free yoga class or buy you lunch.

But the work I've done, and the work I want to help you do, is actually on the *inside*, which is why you *burn-in*—you work on your sense of self and let go of your ego, false sense of control, fear, anger and resentments. You surrender your ideas about how things should be and go beyond the expectations of society, the systems, the way things "ought" to be and you just…be. Be a human being. Every time you experience a negative thought or emotion or get triggered, I encourage you to let go of it, opening more space for you to ignite the fires that will warm and brighten your life from the inside out.

I want to show you that you can be happy *right now*.

There is a piece of this that is financial, and we're going to talk about it. I've long been interested in concepts like FIRE, which stands for Financial Independence, Retire Early. As doctors (and nurses and other people working in the medical field), many of us are making the kind of salaries that make investing smart an option, and that's something I've taken seriously, amassing a 22-million-dollar real estate portfolio in the span of just a few years. I'd be lying if I said money wasn't, in some ways, an antidote to burnout. How many of us work the long hours and shoulder the burdens of running a practice to make money to pay for houses, vacations and the hundreds of thousands of dollars in loans it's easy to amass in medical school?

Maybe that's why you picked up this book in the first place —because you want to learn how to leverage your salary into an even bigger number, one that will let you work less and call the shots more in your day-to-day life. And if that's the case, it's okay. I don't blame you for hoping that changing your financial situation will change the rest of your life because in many ways, it will.

But money is just a part of my life, and it's just a part of yours. I want to help you make more money, but more than that, I want to share with you the tools for changing your mindset, for helping you come to a place of peace, joy and contentment. These are tools for developing the kind of inner life that can't be pummeled by what's going on outside. Because I really, truly believe anyone can do it—and I believe that you don't need to experience having a child with cancer, a health scare of your own or anxiety about a global pandemic to get there. All you need is an open mind.

So, do I have permission to take you on this ride? Are you ready to experience the freedom of burn-*in*?

Let's go!

ONE

Who Am I, and How Did I Get Here?

I sometimes wonder if the universe intended for me to become a doctor—if that was somehow the plan all along.

It certainly seems that way, especially when you look at my family tree. My mother came to the United States from Vietnam during the war. She was only 17 and probably a lot more focused on her goals than the average 17-year-old. While attending college in Long Beach, she had two tasks: one was learning the science she'd need to know to get into medical school, and the other was learning English. By the end of her time as an undergraduate, she was fluent in both biology and the language of her new country, and she moved to the Bay Area to start medical school at the University of California at San Francisco (UCSF). That's also where I come into the story because it's where she met my father.

They had some big things in common. Like my mother, my father was a Vietnamese immigrant—and also like her, he was building a career in health care, training at UCSF as a resident prosthodontist. Medicine was in his blood; his father (my grandfather) was an obstetrician/gynecologist who trained at Johns Hopkins University. Initially, my grandfather's plan was to study in America and then live and work in Vietnam. For a time, that's what he did. Working for the Southern Vietnamese government, he was the minister of health (think *surgeon general*), helping to establish hospitals and clinics and bringing some of what he'd learned in the United States back home.

Eventually, my grandfather found himself working with the World Health Organization, and as part of what must have seemed like a grand adventure to my father and his siblings, the entire family packed up once more and moved to Cameroon. The fledgling African nation was at that time experiencing what's known as a "brain drain": their best and brightest students were traveling to Europe and the United States for higher education. But instead of returning home with their newfound knowledge, they were choosing to live and work abroad. My grandfather's task was to use what he'd learned developing medical infrastructure in Vietnam to help build a medical school that would train Cameroon's future doctors, which would, in turn, encourage them to stay and practice there.

By the time my parents had me, sandwiched between an older sister and a younger brother, they'd settled in Piedmont, a suburb in the East Bay near the city of Oakland and the University of California, Berkeley (Cal). From an early age, I was drawn to science and did especially well in biology. It felt like I was on a straight-shot path to having a "Dr." in front of my name.

After high school, where I continued to do well in science classes, I stayed close to home for college, choosing to study at Cal. But while I was a great student, I also had a huge ego, as evidenced by my high school yearbook. Remember the concept of the senior quote? At the beginning of the year, after taking portraits that would eventually decorate the walls of their parents' homes, high school seniors submit a quote to be printed under their name and photo in the yearbook. It's a short series of words to, in some way, sum up who they were and what they wanted people to think about them. Even though this is usually done in the fall (and college admissions letters don't start appearing in mailboxes until the spring), I had "Berkeley, Class of 2010" printed under my smiling face.

I thought that I was going to go to Berkeley. I *knew* I was going to go to Berkeley. Can you imagine how embarrassed I'd have been if I hadn't gotten in? But the idea that I wouldn't wasn't scary or nerve-racking—it simply wasn't even something I'd considered as a cocky 17-year-old.

Attend Berkeley I did, and from there, I thought the world was my oyster—an opinion reinforced by the fact that I was awarded a merit scholarship to medical school at the University of Michigan in Ann Arbor, a top-10 school I was proud to attend.

I won't say that the world *wasn't* my oyster, but I also won't deny that my system was a bit shocked upon my arrival in Michigan. In high school, I'd been at the top of my class, and though Berkeley is a challenging school, I did well enough there to be ranked at the top of my class, too—I was, if I may put it a little bluntly, *hot shit*.

But at Michigan, *everyone* seemed like hot shit, which in retrospect makes sense—many of my classmates had been at the top of their classes, too, and I think a lot of us were probably used to being the smartest person in any given room. Once classes got underway, I settled in and buckled down. While I had some exposure to life as a doctor via my parents, I wasn't sure which field I wanted to go into, so I kept my eyes open, waiting for the right specialty to reveal itself to me.

During a plastic surgery rotation, I learned about burn reconstruction. Something about it instantly resonated with me. I saw one case where the patient had been burned in a kerosene fire. He had these disfiguring and uncomfortable scars on his hand that prevented him from fully closing it, which made doing any number of daily tasks difficult or impossible.

After an hour in the operating room, through manipulating the scar tissue and rearranging it, we released the adhesions and gave him back his dexterity. I remember my mentor, Paul Cederna, performing multiple Z-plasties, surgeries to open up the contracted scars. With the completion of each one, he would breathe out a sigh, as if feeling relief from the scar's tension himself: "*Ahhhhh.*" It was a beautiful experience to witness. The patient went to sleep unable to use his hand, and when he woke up, it was functional.

I'm going to spoil the next chapter of this book and tell you that today, I don't practice burn reconstruction—in fact, I didn't even stick with plastic surgery. But looking back, I see that from an early age I was drawn to medicine not just because I was good at it but because I saw something powerful in being able to give people the precious tools they need to live their best lives.

———

I come from a big family. I have, as I mentioned, two siblings, and my parents each have their own brothers and sisters. Among my aunts and uncles, there are enough medical professionals to staff a small hospital: a radiologist, a family medicine doctor, two orthopedic surgeons, an otorhinolaryngologist (ENT), a urologist, an ophthalmologist, an internal medicine doctor, an obstetrician/gynecologist, a nuclear medicine doctor, a cardiologist, a radiation-oncologist, an oromaxillofacial surgeon and myself, a dermatologist (plus my own parents —my mother the allergist/immunologist and my father the prosthodontist). Between the 21 cousins on my mom's side of the family and the 15 on my father's, guess how many of us followed in the footsteps of previous generations and went into medicine?

If you guessed more than three, you'd be wrong. Just one cousin on my mother's side is a doctor, with another who recently got into medical school. I'm the only member of my father's extended family that went into what, until our generation, was the family business. My sister is a kindergarten teacher, and my brother has a DMA (Doctor of Musical Arts) —he became another Dr. Tran, just not the kind my mother had hoped for.

How come I'm the only one that got the memo? The question might be better framed as "How come I'm the only one that *didn't* get the memo?" While it's natural for kids to be interested in what their parents do, my siblings, cousins and I all got an up-close look at the lives of doctors and saw things we didn't want for our own adult lives. We saw the stress and the turmoil. We also saw that while in some cases our older relatives might have seemed like they were in positions of power, they were often at the mercy of forces way beyond their control: schedules, administrators, insurance companies, and more—oh, my!

———

I inherited the "doctor gene" from my parents, but I learned recently that it might not be the only thing that was handed down to me.

During my son's battle with cancer, my father had a syncopal episode (he passed out, for any non-doctors reading this) and was rushed to the emergency room. Because they were worried that he might have had a heart attack, they performed an EKG, which showed concerning signs. Luckily, the cardiac catheterization didn't reveal significant blockage, meaning he didn't have a heart attack. However, during an echocardiogram, we learned that he has something called hypertrophic cardiomyopathy, which for him means that one of the walls of his heart is 2.5x thicker than it should be. This occurred not from a poor diet or excessive stress but because of genetics. And if it turns out he does have the specific genetic mutation that causes his heart wall to be an inch thick when it should be ten millimeters, there's a 50 percent chance that I have it, too.

In my father's case, dehydration from a stomach bug put him into a state where his heart didn't have enough blood going into it. When the left ventricle squeezed and tried to push blood out to the body, he had decreased blood flow to the brain because of the thickened wall. That's what made him pass out.

He was lucky: not knowing you have this condition means, for many people, a sudden death. I remember learning about it in medical school. We called it HOCM, or hypertrophic obstructive cardiomyopathy. The classic scenario is there's a seemingly healthy 20-year-old kid playing basketball with his friends. Suddenly and without warning, he collapses and dies.

That could have easily been my father. And if I have the mutation, it could have been me.

When I told some friends about my dad, they were all very sympathetic. "What a year this has been for you and your family," a few of them said. "We're so sorry you're dealing with this."

Here's my response to that:

How lucky am I?

. . .

Seriously! My father is alive. He passed out, went to the hospital and was diagnosed in a matter of days. I have so many doctor friends who made themselves instantly available to answer questions and make referrals.

While this condition can be deadly, it's also manageable: many people do well with just a pill, a beta blocker, and there are surgeries to resect the thickened heart muscle wall and correct the mechanical problem. There's also a newer technique called alcohol septal ablation, where they insert a catheter into the left ventricle and create a controlled heart attack to thin the wall. They can also implant a device that will shock your heart if you go into a weird rhythm (one of the main causes of death in HOCM), the same way a doctor would use paddles. With the right treatment and some luck, my father may live decades longer.

And what about me? How many times in my life have I been out of breath, overheated from intense exercise or wired from partying like there's no tomorrow? I know now that I'll need to get tested and get my son tested so if either one of us carries the mutation, we can keep it under control.

How could I not feel lucky? How could I not marvel at what a miracle it is that I'm still alive and kicking?

———

If I had been dealing with a sick son and a sick father five years ago, I doubt if I could have tapped into the kind of positive mindset that allows me to think about how lucky I am every day and how grateful I am to be who I am, where I am, right now.

I've done a lot of reading, worked with coaches and really pushed myself beyond the limits of my comfort zone to get to this space, which is part of why I'm writing this book. I don't think anyone is born knowing how to navigate the world with hope and gratitude in the face of hardship, and I also don't think it's something you need to make into your whole profession and reason for being.

You might think to reach enlightenment, you must sit under a banyan tree for 49 days or meditate in a cave for 49 years. But don't you have a life to live? The real challenge is finding the grace in your everyday practice. Once you start to consider the possibility that owning your mindset is the most powerful part of being alive, you'll notice examples of it happening all around you.

When I was in high school, pop culture was obsessed with *The Secret*. It was a book and then a movie, and if you're older than 30, I guarantee you've encountered one or the other at some point during your life. I never read the book and only recently saw the movie on Netflix, but I picked up the general idea, which comes from the concept of the law of attraction. If you want something, you must envision it—that's it. The envisioning turns into manifesting, and then you're a movie star or the president or you've won a Nobel Prize or married the girl of your dreams.

I obviously thought that this was utter nonsense. I wasn't at the top of my class because I envisioned being at the top of my class; I was there because I'd worked for it.

But manifestation—true manifestation—is not about skipping the hard work portion of life. As I'm constantly learning, it's about approaching the world with an open mind and an open heart and believing that when you really need something, when you're really meant to have something, it will find you. That by envisioning what you really want, you will prime your reticular activating system in your brainstem to filter your experiences in the world to convert your subconscious desires into a conscious reality. As Tony Robbins says, "Where focus goes, energy flows."

My wife and I recently decided to look for a new house. I

invest heavily in real estate, but I don't invest in single-family homes because you often find yourself competing with emotional buyers who get stuck on "the dream home" and are willing to pay whatever it takes to win the inevitable bidding war.

From a financial standpoint, it doesn't make a ton of sense if you're looking to buy solely as an investment. But suddenly, my wife and I *were* those dream home buyers. We were outgrowing our house, and its placement in a busy neighborhood meant cars were constantly peeling around corners, with screeching tires rattling us at all hours of the day and night. Adrian is a little boy fighting for his life—he needs peace, quiet and space to play. We dreamed about a backyard or maybe even a spa where my wife and I could soak in precious moments of relaxation at the end of a long day.

Deciding to move is one thing, but doing it is quite another. The real estate market is on fire in many parts of the country, and it's definitely on fire where I live in Modesto. I can't tell you how many houses we looked at, hoping each time that we'd found The One. And when we thought we'd found it, we worried about being chosen. It's not unheard of for houses in our area to field offers from a dozen buyers within a week of hitting the market.

When we found the place that felt like the home we were meant to live in as a family, we wrote a letter to the sellers. We talked about Adrian and what he'd been going through and about how his illness had brought us closer as a family—how it made us understand the beauty and the magic of life.

We explained that their home was one we could see ourselves thriving in, living, working and playing as a happy, loving family. We shared our dream that this home would be the place where our son would feel comfort, joy and healing during this challenging time. We attached a few pictures so they could put faces to the voices in our letter.

Then, we waited. Was I nervous? Of course! There are no guarantees in real estate, and as an investor, I've learned how to emotionally detach from properties and transactions. At the same time, I felt a sense of calm wash over me when I thought about this house. I felt in my bones that this was going to be our home. That it *was* our home.

We moved in recently, and in chatting with the seller Randi, I learned about an incredible moment of serendipity.

"When we purchased the home, we did the same thing!" She told me. "We added a picture of our family and we wrote a letter. Your offer was the only one that came in with a letter and a picture."

As I was feeling my connection to the house strengthen, Randi was experiencing something similar. "When my husband and I first bought the house," she said, "we were kind of newly starting our family together. And we wanted to find a home that had space to grow. And we got a lot out of that house as a *home*, not just a house. When we got your offer and it had this picture of your family and this story about what your family was experiencing and what you were looking for in a home and how you connected with our home, we felt like we were passing the home onto the next family who could grow and connect to it the same way we did, because it was more than just a house for us."

We've only been moved in a short time—at the time of this writing, we're not even fully unpacked yet! There are still boxes on the floor in the kitchen, but the house has already become a *home* for my family, too.

It wasn't the first house we put in a bid on. Earlier in the process, we'd made an offer on a house that looked remarkably like the one in which we now live, with one key difference: it had hard, cold marble floors. This was an aesthetically popular choice, sure, but recall that we have a fragile young son who also happens to be in the crash-into-everything stage of toddlerhood. The home we live in now has carpeted floors —a soft place to land for the littlest member of our family.

The house we live in also has another one of our wish-list items: a backyard spa. As busy and as hectic as life is, we've still found time to use it, getting so much joy from being able to soak away a hard day, floating in the water as the sun sets.

Now, do I think the universe is handing out backyard spas to anyone who wants one? Maybe not. But I do think—I know —that there's real power in choosing to see yourself as the creator of your own life. In actively working to shape your own destiny and seeing your hard work not as mere work but as part of a life that looks the way you want it to. The way you believe it can look. That what you want and what you get are reflections of who you are and how you move through the world. In building, one positive thought at a time, your very own dream house.

———

Not a lot of people know that the sculptor Michelangelo didn't create the statue of David—one of his most famous works—from a raw block of marble. Decades before he was even born, a group of wealthy Italian patrons commissioned another artist to render the biblical figure in marble. He gave up halfway through the carving process, and over the years a number of other artists attempted to finish what had been started.

Only Michelangelo, when he took over the project in 1521, had the vision to complete the story. Where other people saw a block of raw marble or a half-finished statue that wasn't that great to begin with, he saw his destiny waiting to be brought to life. He saw his future and he saw himself carving it, sure in the knowledge that the result would be a masterpiece.

Be the creator of your own life. Chisel it out of marble and treat it like the precious work of art that it is.

TWO

Where Am I Going?

Becoming a doctor isn't for the faint of heart.

Let's say you make it to medical school. You'll be doing work that is equivalent in difficulty to upper-level college biology courses, things like biochemistry and genetics. But instead of learning the material in a semester, you'll be expected to master it in a week.

Then, you'll have to do it again the next week and the week after that. It is a volume overload of information. In many instances, you'll be pitted against your classmates. You'll spend all your time with the same group of people—in no small part because there's not really time to develop a social life outside of school—but the relationships won't always be congenial. Usually, the first two years of school aren't as competitive in pass/no pass programs, but if you're awarded honors or high pass for greater levels of achievement after that, then I wish you luck. Once you move into clinical rotations, the pressure to outshine fellow students intensifies.

It's still a tight-knit group—you'll have study groups, and people will want to help each other. But you'll also be aware that some of the people in your cohort are *not*, as they say on

reality television, there to make friends. There are stories of
"gunners," slang for the med students trying to beat everyone
on the curve, ripping out pages from library textbooks to sabo-
tage fellow students. I didn't experience that directly, but I've
seen enough to know that it's a very real phenomenon.

I was that guy once, even though it was totally uninten-
tional! I was reading a lot in my pediatrics rotation, and I
pissed off my friend, another medical student, because I spoke
up during his patient presentation. I made the residents feel
bad about themselves because I was insecure and trying to
demonstrate my knowledge; suddenly I was the bad guy, even
though it was not my intention to hurt people's feelings.

Which brings me to another thing I had to learn—sometimes the hard way—in medical school. For so long, my life
had been about tests, grades and projects. Absorbing huge
quantities of material and then showing my professors and
myself that I knew it better than anyone else. I won't say it
wasn't incredibly important work, or that knowledge isn't a
huge part of being successful in college and in medical school.

But training as a doctor in a clinical setting is a different
world with different rules. Now, you're not just focused on
being the smartest person in the room or just studying and
taking exams. You're working *with* your team instead of
against your classmates. You need communication skills, a
bedside manner and other soft skills that maybe you didn't
hone while studying 14 hours a day. It's not enough to just be
the smartest guy. You have to be the nicest guy. The most
helpful guy. Now you have to do all the scut work for residents
so they'll like you and want to help you advance.

And I didn't get it. Science always came naturally to me,
but for this part of being a doctor, I didn't understand the
game. Because it truly is a game that you play when you're
rotating. In a hospital, a medical student is not especially
useful to anyone around them. What you have to do, if you

want to excel in your clinical rotations, is make the resident's life easier.

Because you are limited in your scope of knowledge and practice as a trainee, it is challenging to directly help a patient. Your job, then, becomes to help the team. While you can advocate for your patients, you can also relieve the work load for the resident physician. Then, your resident will pass on a good word on to the attending, and you'll get a good evaluation.

In a lot of ways, it's about surrender. About giving up control. My first few years of medical school, our lectures were recorded, so I didn't attend them live. I'd watch it on double speed at home whenever I felt like it. I would eat what I wanted, when I wanted, and I'd go to martial arts or the gym twice a day. But then, when it came time to do hospital rotations, I had to be there at 4 am on the dot to pre-round for surgery before the sun was up. And it just sucks. You don't have control of your own time, your own space.

You're being, in a sense, broken down so that you can be built back up as a doctor. The first job for most medical students doing surgery rotations is to cut a suture with scissors. They hand you scissors, and your hands are shaking because you're nervous, and the surgeon is a tough guy ready to come down on you if you make one wrong move. You're on edge, palms sweating, thinking: *Am I going to do this right? Am I going to get yelled at? Is this cut going to impact the trajectory of my career for the rest of my life?*

Over a *cut*. And not even a cut of an actual patient's skin or muscle—a suture! Cutting is something I've known how to do most of my life. It's a skill they teach in kindergarten. And here I was, in the equivalent of the 20th grade, afraid that a skill I mastered a good 20 years ago might suddenly fail me and derail all the work I'd done up to that point.

Now I wonder: why does it have to be like that? Why do

some doctors have to be jerks? Is it just in a surgeon's nature?
Is it because they were trained in this way, and therefore now
you must train in the same way and suffer the same torture?
Why do they have to make you so nervous? What's the root of
this culture of embarrassment? Because it's very real. Quizzes
and exams aren't just graded individually, privately. You're
roasted in front of your class! Let's say there's four of you
rotating on surgery and the attending takes you all aside and
asks, "Okay, what exits the inferior vena cava at this point?
Which side of the aorta comes off first to the kidney, the left
or the right renal artery?"

Or "What are the common causes of pancreatitis? Oh,
great job, you said scorpion sting? Which species of scorpion?" And there's a race to answer, to make sure the attending
knows that out of the four students, you're the one who *deserves*
to be there. They have a not-so-pleasant term for this line of
questioning, one that also reflects some of the macho energy
(regardless of gender) floating around these spaces: they call it
"pimping." The surgeon demands answers to clinically rele-
vant anatomy or etiology questions or sometimes just quizzes
you on random factoids like "Why are flamingos pink?" or
"Which '80s musician is responsible for this terrible song I
insist on playing in the operating room whenever I'm
performing a major surgery?"

It's impressive for medical students to be able to answer
the surgeon's question, and there were plenty of instances in
which I had the right answer. But for me, medical school was
also an exercise in learning to understand—and overcome—
cultural differences between me and many of the people I was
working with and learning from.

I come from an Asian family, and in Asian culture, children are seen and not heard. It's considered respectful if
you're quiet and reserved and don't make too much of a
scene. What's valued in Western medicine, or in medicine in

general, is somebody who will speak up and who is confident. If you're quiet, some people might think that you aren't knowledgeable, that you aren't paying attention, or that you're not a team player. If you're not culturally trained to shout out the answer *because you were raised to think shouting out answers is rude*, then you will never seem smart, even though you do know the answer.

I struggled with this a lot. I was a product of my upbringing, which meant I was quiet. I was shy, and it took me a long time to find my voice and my confidence. I had to learn to speak up when I knew the answer and when I saw something that wasn't right. I had been taught for so long not to rock the boat or step on anyone's toes, but that wasn't serving me as a medical student or as a person the more I engaged with the world outside of school.

––––––

I matched at Indiana University in a great (and extremely competitive) program of integrated plastic and reconstructive surgery. For six years, it would be where I'd hone my skills, learn everything I needed to know about plastic surgery and become a master of reconstructive burn surgery.

A lot of burn surgery is acute care. If somebody gets burned in a fire, the work surgeons do literally keeps them alive. It's skin grafting, critical care, fluid management. The operations are not pretty little flaps—they are massive skin grafts in a hot operating room. You're surrounded by people: the anesthesiologist, the residents, the scrub techs, the perioperative nurses, the care team after in the ICU.

I could see that while I might eventually be captain of the ship, I wouldn't necessarily have total control over my work. I would, however, bear tremendous responsibility: imagine a 20-year-old kid burned in a fiery car crash and me talking to his family about pulling the plug because even if he were to survive, it would be a miserable existence where he would be in constant pain, unable to walk, eat, move or breathe on his own.

For so long, working as a burn surgeon had been central to my conception of who I was, what I was meant to be doing and where my life was going.

And I was miserable.

I remember thinking: *is this what I signed up for?*

I just wanted to escape. It was so bad that I remember, at one point, thinking, *I should just jump off the top floor of this parking garage and be out of it.* That was a dark moment. I've never had major depressive disorder. As a physician, I know all the diagnostic criteria for clinical depression.

Looking back, I can say that it probably wasn't a true moment of suicidal ideation—I don't think I would have actually done it. But just because I wasn't in the kind of crisis that might have required admission to a psych ward doesn't mean it's something I can brush off when I think about that time in my life. It wasn't right. It's not a healthy thought to want to end your life by jumping off a parking garage, but it's one that doctors, dentists and other health-care professionals are all too familiar with.

In 2018, the American Psychiatry Association released a decade-long study that discovered between 300 and 400 doctors die by suicide every year—a number that, per 100,000 people, is double that of the non-medical population. While I'm grateful that my own mental health struggles weren't as severe as what some of our colleagues experience, part of my mission now is confronting doctor burnout head-on in the hopes that we as a community can push back against the suffering that goes hand in hand with the job for so many of us.

What I was searching for during that time was escape. I

even emailed an old pathology professor from medical school, thinking that maybe a specialty where I didn't interact with patients at all would be less taxing mentally and emotionally. It's no less challenging a specialty, but I did hear from the people I talked with that their pathology department regularly fielded inquiries from burned-out residents looking to escape clinical medicine.

I didn't actually want to be a pathologist, but I had another idea.

Before matching into plastic surgery, I had considered going into dermatology. The hours are good, the pay is good and you're less likely to encounter the kinds of emergencies I was dealing with as a burn surgeon. What held me back, though, was what I thought plastic surgery offered: the opportunity to change someone's life in the operating room. That's what I wanted to do.

I loved the geometry of the work: designing a perfect flap, performing a seamless reconstruction. In my plastic surgery training, I was being taught to do a wide variety of procedures —everything from fixing a cleft lip to hand and breast reconstructive surgery. As an intern, I had the rare privilege of touching and protecting a two-year-old's brain during a joint case with neurosurgery to reshape a prematurely fused skull known as craniosynostosis. But I was realizing, the more I thought about it, that I didn't want to do every type of surgery. What I wanted was to master a few operations—and to do them very often and very well.

Plastics and dermatology often overlap, so it wasn't difficult for me to become acquainted with the chair of the dermatology department, Steve Wolverton, whose name carries some clout as he authored a well-known pharmacology textbook. One day, I told him, "I don't think that I'm happy in plastic surgery. I think I'm supposed to be a dermatologist." He took me under his wing, which ultimately led me to a dermatology residency in Washington, DC, where I picked up a newly opened spot at Howard University Hospital that was generously funded by the Veterans Affairs Medical Center. From there, I returned to my home state of California, completing a fellowship in what I currently specialize in: Mohs micrographic surgery.

It's a procedure in which I cut somebody's skin cancer off their nose or ear, on their face or another high-risk area, and then I check the margins myself under the microscope and see if I got all the cancer or not. Then, once I've removed the cancer, I do the reconstruction. It's the perfect hybrid of dermatology and what I initially loved about plastic surgery. I do all the same reconstructive operations with beautiful flaps to restore somebody's nose, their contour and its breathing functions after a big cancer is removed. It was really what excited me in plastic surgery to begin with. It wasn't all the bigger surgeries but the local flaps and procedures that were faster paced. You can do a DIEP microsurgery for bilateral breast reconstruction, and it can take 20 hours.

The reconstructive surgeries I do after skin cancer take maybe 10 or 20 minutes. It was a better match for my person-ality. I was still doing important, life-changing work, but it was the kind of work I could finish in a morning or an afternoon. When a patient comes to see me, they leave the same day, transformed in a powerful way.

Leaving plastic surgery wasn't something I took lightly. Once the idea took shape, I talked to people who had been where I was, asking plastic surgeons further along in their careers if they were happy and if, given the chance to do it all over, they'd make the same choices. A lot of them were candid with me and said, "Probably not."

One doctor, Adam, said to me, "I'm 55 years old, and I don't have a family. I don't have a wife. I don't have kids. Going back, did I make the right decisions? I don't know."

I talked to another plastic surgeon, Bill, the father of one of the residents I rotated with in medical school back in Michigan, and he told me a similar story. He had a wife and kids, and his son was a plastic surgery resident. He said, "You know what, Patrick? I didn't spend a lot of time with my children when they were young, and so I feel like I missed out on them growing up. That is something that I regret."

This was years before I met my wife and years before my son was born, but they are such a huge part of my life and my world now—two people that bring me joy and fulfillment beyond measure. And yet, had I not listened to the part of me that knew I wasn't on the path I was meant to be walking, they might not be here with me now. It's a sobering fact, one that makes me incredibly grateful I had the opportunity to change my life so dramatically and also grateful that I listened to my intuition, tuning out all the outside noise to focus instead on what I really needed to learn.

———

Have you ever gone to a seafood restaurant, grocery store or even just the beach and seen a bunch of crabs stuck in a barrel together? You don't have to place a lid on it. The crabs will never escape. They're all trying to pull each other down. An individual crab will never escape from the box because as soon as he gains a little height, another crab will grab him with its pincers and pull him back down. Crabs don't know any better, but humans do. Instead of acting like crabs in a barrel, so desperate to keep people beneath us no matter what, what if we worked together to get out of the damn barrel?

Wherever you go, extend kindness to the people who are learning around you, behind you and in front of you.

THREE

The Victim Mindset

If you ask almost anyone who *isn't* a doctor, they'll tell you almost certainly that doctors are successful people and that to be a doctor, you have to be smart, hardworking and driven. Perhaps more importantly to some, doctors can make a lot of money, which is, for better or worse, the most common definition of success in our society.

So many people think doctors make a ton of money, and sure, on paper a lot of us do. But health- care costs in America have risen exponentially, and doctor's salaries haven't even kept up with inflation. It's the insurance companies, hospital administrators and pharmaceutical industries who are really reaping the profits. Doctors have poor representation because they're not as active in lobbying as other groups, which makes them an easy scapegoat. So, too, does the consistent media portrayal of the "rich doctor" stereotype.

In reality, a lot of doctors mismanage money and live paycheck to paycheck—like the college kid who makes it to the NFL and signs a $20 million a year contract and then goes bankrupt when he tears his ACL. Why does that happen? Because nobody taught him the wealth mindset. He was rich

—with a poor mindset. He was taken advantage of by his managers, so-called friends and family.

Doctors are also often targets for shark insurance salesmen who will sell them expensive life insurance they don't want or need at prices they can't afford, only to make the highest commission possible for the agent. Contractors or other people who work for you will charge extra when they find out you're a doctor because they think you can stomach it and are not that financially savvy.

Even doctors who appear outwardly successful aren't set up for success. How many of us actually learned how to manage money or run a practice or deal with burnout in medical school or residency? I'd argue that medical school and residency teach you to do the opposite of those things—they teach you how to be overworked, how to not have control of your own time and mental energy, and, for a lot of people, how to be broke.

Add those years to the very real burdens a lot of us face in our careers, and suddenly it seems very easy—and very comfortable—to feel like a victim in your own life. As you look at other people, your ego wants to protect itself, and so you silently seethe while looking at your peers, thinking (for example): *he's successful because his parents were both doctors*, or *he didn't have student loans to pay because his parents helped him with school*, or *she's doing well because her husband makes a lot of money, so she can take these low-paying fellowships and not worry about paying rent.*

They can be successful, but I can't be. I'm stuck with loans I'll never pay back. My specialty is too competitive. I'll never get a good job. I'll never get that promotion. Who am I to practice medicine? I'm not good enough. I hope they don't figure out that I'm a fraud, an impostor. That I don't know what I'm doing and I don't deserve any of this. That I'm not worthy.

Are any of these things true, though? Or are they convenient stories we tell ourselves to soothe our egos when we feel powerless? I want to challenge you: what would your life look like if you dropped that story? What if you stopped asking yourself why these things happen to you? What if you began asking how these things are happening *for* me? What if you told a new story, one in which you don't just survive being a doctor but actually thrive? What would happen if you stopped being a victim and started taking ownership of your life?

If there's one thing that I've learned from the challenges in my life, it's this: if I'm going to bitch and moan it, then I'd better own it. When I started to take ownership of my life, everything changed dramatically and got significantly better. Your son may not have cancer, but I can promise you that you will experience suffering and strife in your life. And when you hit that threshold of struggle, what questions will you ask?

Life is not fair. Sometimes it provides you unfair advantages, and sometimes it offers injustices that make you want to rebel. The only thing I know for sure is that you will have pain in your life.

When you bitch and moan about your situation, remember to own your situation. Because when you change your questions, you change your life.

———

A lot of us are burned out for one simple reason: it's just the sheer number of years of training. Most people graduate from high school. That's 12 years of school. Some of those people graduate college, which adds another four. For doctors? Double it. I went to the equivalent of 25th grade! It's that much more systematic indoctrination and loss of control over your own time, especially as a medical student, where you're drinking from a firehose of information.

So, let's say you match—which, by the way, is getting harder and harder. Last year, the *New York Times* published an article about the rise in medical school graduates who don't match—not because they aren't worthy of becoming residents but because there are now way more medical school graduates than there are actual residency spots. That means people who have $300,000 in debt find themselves unable to work in the field for which they've gone to school—despite a chronic nationwide doctor shortage!

For our purposes, we'll assume you've matched. I've talked a little bit about my experience in residency, and it might be easy to brush that off as a "me" problem—as something I experienced because I was in the wrong specialty. It's likely, though, that I would have had a hard time in any residency program because residency, for lack of a more elegant way to put it, *sucks*.

You clock in 80 hours a week, taking care of patients, studying and trying not to mess up. There are personality conflicts with colleagues and bosses, many of whom have a unique ability to make you, an objectively smart person, feel incredibly stupid. You're also probably getting paid very little money.

When I was a resident in Washington, DC my salary was so low that I qualified for affordable housing. I was lucky not to also be facing a ton of debt, but for people who are, every year they aren't earning good money intensifies the pressure. Those 80-hour weeks also don't allow you the time to learn the life management skills many of our peers start to master as soon as they finish college. People in our profession also don't go around advertising their net worth. Professors don't talk about the money that they make. Students whose parents are bankrolling them aren't encouraged to make that fact known. It's frowned upon to talk about money, and that hurts all of us in the long run.

I didn't get a credit card until I was done with medical school, which means that yes, I avoided falling into the "spend more than you have" trap, but it also means I spent years not building credit—putting me further away from my financial goals. We also just don't talk about money enough.

The idea goes that people want to become doctors because they want to *help*, to do good for society. I want to do good for society, but I also want to live in a house and provide for my family. Nowhere in medical school are we talking enough about the financial realities of being a doctor—what a strong job offer and salary looks like compared to workload, how to run a practice efficiently, how to prioritize paying off student debt versus investing for the future and so on. It's not just money, either—so much of my life as a student and as a resident was about getting by when I was capable, as I now know, of so much more.

———

For many people who make it through the gauntlet of medical school, residency and even further training, the easiest option is to take a job working for a large medical conglomerate—I won't name names here, but you can probably guess the places I'm talking about.

This work can be incredibly appealing for people who have spent the last decade being told what to do and when to do it because it's more of the same. You're a W2 employee, you get to work when they tell you to get to work and you see whatever patients they assign to you. You get, in short, what you get. The salary is exciting—how could it not be after spending so much time scrimping and saving to get by? You're not thinking about the fact that you don't really know how to use it, how to invest it or how to spend it unless you've been doing research on the outside. And we know, when you're in medical school or residency, how much time there is for outside interests (if you're not a doctor and you happen to be reading this book, the answer is "none").

You're set up for failure, in my opinion, because nobody

teaches you about finances. They teach you to be a doctor, but you can't just be a doctor because now, medicine is truly a business. That's why health-care costs have risen exorbitantly. That's why the administrators are taking huge cuts from you. That's why there's so much insurance pushback.

Money, though, is an integral part of living. It's not like you're a monk living off people's donations. You must work to live. You must do everything for yourself. You must make it to support your family and pay off the hundreds of thousands of dollars in student loans that you've been avoiding. You're also a doctor, and it's easy to fall down the rabbit hole of spending what you think you're entitled to spend. *Why shouldn't I have a nice car?* you might wonder. *Why shouldn't I buy my wife that diamond tennis bracelet or sign my kids up for private horseback riding lessons?* I'm not here to shame you about whatever it is you spend your money on—that's your choice! I am here to point out that *way* too many doctors are living paycheck to paycheck, which in turn keeps them working more hours in jobs that make them miserable.

After the bloom of making money wears off—and trust me, it does wear off—you start to get pissed off about things that you don't expect, like the amount of paperwork attached to even the simplest patient visits. There's a whole bureaucracy that you don't understand, and then you start to create adversarial relationships—not only with your patients (who can piss you off when they don't listen to you) but also with your employer when you don't see things eye to eye. When you, the doctor, are overruled by an administrator who wouldn't last a day in your shoes.

You don't understand why you can't have everything you want, like why you can't get paid more money, why you don't have more support staff, why you have to work these long hours. And the reality is all of those are still your choices. It's not like you were forced to accept one contract over another or forced to work in any particular place. But you thought you were. You thought that this was it.

It's no wonder, then, that so many doctors get stuck in what I call the victim mindset. They feel sorry for themselves, like it's too late to make a change. From there, it's a slippery slope to a bitterness that radiates outward—your family feels it, your coworkers feel it and your patients feel it.

On paper, doesn't that sound nuts? We're some of the most educated people in the country and plenty of us are making over or multiples of six figures every year. Why do we feel so put-upon, so exhausted, so *burnt out?*

A lot of the hospitals and administrators don't get it. How many emails have you gotten encouraging you to drink more water and get more exercise? That doesn't work. It's slapping a Band-Aid on a bullet wound, and all the free yoga classes or 7 pm "cheers to our medical heroes" in the world aren't going to stop you from bleeding to death.

So, what do we do?

I think that the answer, ultimately, comes from within. It comes from taking responsibility. From recognizing that there is so much in this world that we can't control, but that there are so, so many things we have the miraculous freedom to get to choose.

Think about all the stuff in your house. How much of it do you want? How much of it do you need or use on a daily basis? This isn't a Marie Kondo thing—I'm not going to tell you to clean out your garage to find inner peace. But how much of the stuff in your house is stuff you bought to impress other people? That you bought because you thought you "should" have it? Imagine how much lighter you'd feel if you only spent money on things that genuinely made you feel good with no input from anyone else. Yeah, you might have less shiny stuff, but what would you have more of?

I live in Modesto, about an hour and a half inland of San Francisco. It's not what anyone would call a bustling metropolis, and as someone who has always lived in big cities or fancy college towns, moving here was a big adjustment. I don't have access to incredible fine dining or opera or a huge community of people who think the way I do.

What I do have is more patients because there are fewer dermatologists in the area for me to compete with and therefore a greater demand for my skillset. I also have a bigger house where my son can run around and play, and my wife and I can relax and host our families and friends. I have grateful patients—people who come to me and are appreciative to be in my office. So, am I going to complain about living in Modesto? Well, I shouldn't! I *chose* to live here, and there are trade-offs in anything in life. The trade-off, for me, was worth it. Here in Modesto with my family, I feel like I'm waking up every day and choosing the life I live.

I don't want the takeaway from this chapter to be that to stop feeling like a victim, you have to move to Modesto. This wouldn't have been the right choice for everyone. Maybe what gives you purpose is living within walking distance of a museum or a zoo or living in the mountains in a cabin without electricity. I want the takeaway to be this: you have the freedom to create and cultivate a beautiful life of your own choosing.

Like so much of what I've come to believe, I look back at my life and see that the power of choice was knocking on my door long before I actually answered.

———

At Berkeley, I taught chemistry as a sophomore. My freshman year, I took Chem 1A. It's a weeder course, which means of the 1,500 of us who took it, more than half were expected to drop out. It was a sink-or-swim environment where if you didn't swim, you were going to fail your course. You were going to get a D or an F. Nobody was holding anyone's hand.

It was too big a school for anyone to give the kind of detailed attention I was used to as a kid who had gone to very good schools with small class sizes.

After the first semester of chemistry, if you want to continue in the pre-med curriculum, then you take Organic Chemistry. Maybe 900 kids finish Chem 1A, and then 800 go on to Organic Chemistry. Half of them drop out by the second semester. Basically, it's a great halving. You're halved at every step of the way until it's the cream of the crop—like a Bitcoin worth a million bucks at the end of it all. There's no number cap, though—all 1,500 kids, if they have the drive, if they have the hustle, if they study hard enough, could pass or even get As.

People have different ideas of what they want in college. Some people get trapped by party culture and want to rush frats and drink a lot. Some people felt pressured by their parents to do pre-med when what they really wanted to do was study poetry. There are probably a million reasons that not everyone could get an A, even though everyone has the potential. Everyone, in a sense, has the choice.

Just because you want something, or think you want something, doesn't mean that you deserve it or that you're meant to have it. You deserve it once you get through the grit. You don't deserve to make a beautiful meal if you haven't put in the hours to hone your craft, and there's no shame in wanting to order takeout instead.

I did well in general chemistry and cruised through it. I did the work required, but it was the minimum work. I didn't spend a lot of time outside of class studying because I had a good grasp of the material already. If I had wanted to do more than what it took to get by, I'd have options. Students at Berkeley have a lot of access to the professors, whether they're going to in-person lectures, watching online or both. Then there are tutors that are freely available, undergrads who have already finished the chemistry course and can provide help.

Not thinking I needed to avail myself of these resources, I phoned it in for general chemistry and did well. I got an A. My second semester, I did organic chemistry. I treated it the same way as general chemistry because, I thought, *I'm a smart kid—I've proven it. Doing the bare minimum got me an A first semester, so why should this be any different?*

That was a rude awakening for me. I'd never done organic chemistry prior to coming to Berkeley, so I had no real framework for the material, and I couldn't phone it in. It was all new knowledge, all new information. Yeah, I was smart, but that's not enough when you're being flooded with molecules and retrosynthesis that might as well be in another language.

My first midterm, I got the worst grade I'd ever seen in my entire life. I was an A student my whole life, and my first semester at Berkeley, I got a 3.95 average. I got an A-minus in my music class because I just phoned it in there, and I didn't work hard. I was pissed off, and I blamed the instructor, my music partner, the material—everyone and everything except myself. I didn't take ownership of my own work, and I couldn't see that I didn't deserve an A.

Back in Organic Chemistry, I wasn't just annoyed about my grade—I was shocked. In bright red ink on my exam was 115/155, and for the first time ever, I was a C student. It was a huge wake-up call. Again, I wanted to blame other people. I said, "My instructor's not good." It's very easy to put the blame on others. It's a lot more challenging when you have to take ownership of it yourself.

After I got my horrifying grade, the instructor, in his melodic French accent, said, "I'm going to write down the initials of the people who got the highest score on the exam." So it was A. J., 153 out of 155. Then the second highest score was J. S., 151. I thought, *Man, that is the caliber of student that I have been in my life. That is what I deserve. How do I get there?*

I emailed the graduate student instructor and said, "Hey, I

didn't do as well as I had hoped on my exam. How do I get the high score?"

She replied with one sentence: "Do practice problems."

So, I did practice problems! Instead of phoning it in, I did all the homework and then some. I read the textbook and taught myself. I did every practice problem, and when I couldn't figure something out, I would ask for help. I would go to the tutor. I would read the text again. I would look at another problem and see if I could parallel it. I would go to office hours.

On the second midterm, I didn't get the highest score, but I did get the second highest. My graduate student was very proud of me—I had gone from being a C student in the middle of the pack to an A+ student back where I thought I belonged, at the top of the pack.

That's what showed me. It's not about your talent, and it's not about what you think you're entitled to. I could have been satisfied with my C-level midterm score—it was a passing grade, one that would have let me continue on to the next semester. I could have been mad about it and stayed mad, ignoring my own responsibility for the grade. I could have—as a lot of people do—let it fester inside, turning me from an excited and eager student into a kid who was bitter and burned out before he even finished undergrad.

What I learned, aside from a lot about organic chemistry, is that I was and am an active participant in my own life. I woke up and made the choice to take the class seriously, just like I woke up and made the choice to switch fields, to move to Modesto and to write this book.

If you feel burned out, does the world need to change in order for you to stop feeling the burnout? Because if you're going to wait for the world to change to accommodate you and make you feel less burned out, you're out of luck. Partly because the world doesn't revolve around you, and partly because even when things outside do change, you're still you.

So many people think, "First, I must have this thing, and then I'll do this thing, and then I'll be happy." It's have, do, be. Once you have a million dollars, then you'll take a vacation and then be happy. Or once you have $10 million, then you'll retire and then you'll be happy.

But guess what? If you're making $300,000 a year and you're unhappy, you're not going to be substantially happier making $1,000,000 or $10,000,000. Having billions of dollars does not change who you are or where you are. No matter where you go and no matter how much money you have, you don't fundamentally change who you are. And if we accept that to be true, we have to ask ourselves: what will more money actually do? What, at the end of the day, is the point?

I think it's this: start from the inside out. Burnout comes from the outside in. It's pressure other people place on you; it's systems you can't control; it's playing a game you'll never win. Burning in, on the other hand, is about nurturing the fire inside. It's about tending to that fire, twig by twig and branch by branch, until it's roaring strong enough to warm you and show you the light of what you're meant to be and where you're meant to go.

———

A lit candle, left to its own devices, will burn out. It's a tenuous flame, subject to being extinguished by any little thing—a gentle breeze, the close of the door or someone walking by too quickly. Rocked by the external world, the candle blows out and dies, and to light it again you have to start over from the very beginning. It would be easier, if your flame went out, to simply stay in the dark forever.

But if you treat the gentle flame that is your soul as a sacred fire, and care for it and love it and fuel it with paper, wood or rocket fuel, it grows stronger. So strong that before you know it, you'll be shining hot and bright enough to keep an entire house full of people cozy and warm. You'll be able to see clearly. All from the starting point of a single candle whose flame kept burning even through the darkest of nights.

Tend to your candle from the inside out. Your flame cannot be extinguished by a draft or a storm. The more you protect it, the stronger it will burn.

FOUR

Here and Now

At one point early in my career, I considered joining a start-up. It was a good idea—one I'd had myself, actually—rooted in the service on-demand model so popular in Silicon Valley (think Uber for Botox). After doing some research, I discovered another doctor had already set something similar into motion, and after a few conversations, he made it clear I'd be more than welcome to become part of his lean team.

In the end I moved on to another opportunity, but the experience taught me something that has been at the foundation of what I've accomplished over the last few years: I am an entrepreneur. It took some time to realize it and a little more time to embrace it, but now I can't imagine living any other way.

You know who else is an entrepreneur? My mother. She was the first doctor and one of the first real estate investors I knew. Her business was local, consisting of single-family homes that she could easily drive to.

Renting single-family homes can be a win-win situation. The tenant is happy because they have a nice place to live and don't have to put down $60,000 to own the place. In turn, they don't have to deal with a $10,000 expense when the roof leaks or a $5,000 charge when the air conditioning needs to be fixed. The landlord receives many benefits as well, including having a tenant pay down their mortgage and increasing their net worth through an increase of equity in the property over time. It's not always that easy, though.

Landlords put themselves in a vulnerable position because *they* are the ones who have to put down $60,000 to take on the loan. They are responsible for paying the debt. If the tenant stops paying, breaks all the windows or clogs the toilets, who is on the hook? The landlord.

And my mom had some less-than-ideal experiences! I'm not sure how she was screening tenants (or if she was screening tenants). I know she dealt with renters who didn't pay, who trashed her assets (turning them into liabilities) and whose demands meant she had to spend a lot more time at her properties than she probably would have liked to.

As an aside—how crazy is it that I remember all of this so vividly? Things I saw and experienced when I couldn't have been more than 10 years old are now sense memories for me, ones that have remained so strong that when I first started buying rental properties, I knew I had to hire a property manager without even thinking about it.

My mom's properties were all in California, and they were all single-family homes—no out-of-state investing, no multi-family units, no commercial properties, triple net lease properties, no strip malls, no medical facilities, no office buildings (all things I've done in the last year, incidentally).

She was—and still is—a boss. Both of my parents speak fluent Vietnamese, English and French, and it was important to them that in addition to thriving in school, we also learned about where they came from—where *we* came from. How can you preserve the home country's traditions and language when you're in a new world?

An ocean separated my parents from their homeland, and I can't imagine the culture shock they must have experienced when they came here and had to learn not just a new language but also new cultural norms and values—even how to stand in lines the "American" way. But I believe America is the only place where my parents would have been able to achieve everything they've achieved.

It's your birthright in America to pursue freedom, happiness, liberty and love. It's your birthright in America to give your children everything you want them to have, which is also something my parents did for us. They helped me pay my tuition at Berkeley, and I lived at home most of the time I went there—how lucky was I to be able to have their support? I spent my first year in the dorms and realized that while dorm life might have been a huge part of *someone's* college experience, it wasn't going to be a huge part of mine. I went back to live with my family in our home, and I rented a parking spot on campus for a fraction of what I'd have paid to live there all four years.

This is perhaps a long-winded way of saying that real estate, like medicine, is something that has been part of my life and part of my journey since before I even knew what or who I wanted to be. It felt natural to come back to it years after I watched my mom begin to invest in single-family homes, though I knew my path would look a little different than hers had.

Part of my reason for moving to Modesto was that unlike Mountain View, where I did my fellowship, you can actually live comfortably there without also being a tech millionaire. I bought my first house in the fall of 2019 just after Adrian was born—we brought him home to our tiny one-bedroom apartment and quickly realized we needed more room to stretch our limbs as we got used to life as a family of three.

Owning that house, which we lived in until recently, was

like being bitten by a bug—the real estate bug. In the winter of 2020, I signed up for a class by Leti and Kenji on investing with a focus on real estate for doctors. I've always been interested in finance blogs, so I jumped into the material with gusto. So much gusto that I didn't actually finish because I felt certain I could figure it out on my own. Life, as they say, got in the way. Suddenly, it was a few months later and I got an email:

"Hey! Have you bought a property yet?"

I had been so gung-ho the first round that it had kept me from slowing down and taking the steps to get to the next level, which in my case was buying my first income-producing property.

I decided I was going to take the course again and do it right this time (which I didn't finish—but at least I took action on it), and by August of 2020, I'd closed on my first property —my first four properties, as it happened, because if I was in for a penny, I figured, I might as well be in for a pound. I had the down payments for them from my previous investing, most of which were held in stock and cryptocurrency. Instead of having all my money in equities, the majority of which were held in low-cost index funds, I sold a lot of it and started investing in more diverse properties. This was better for me tax-wise, and it had more potential for me to accelerate my growth.

That's when I started grinding. That's when I started calling all the realtors. That's when I hit the market. That's when I read more books about real estate, got online and found communities of other people like me who had the same goals. In October 2020, I joined a business coaching group and met a CRNA named Matt during a discussion of FIRE principles. FIRE, as I mentioned before, stands for Financial Independence, Retire Early. The idea is that during your prime working years, you're stashing away as much cash as possible and funneling it toward your preferred investment vehicle.

If you make $100,000 a year, let's say, FIRE aficionados might suggest you live on half of that and get the rest of it working. Eventually, when you reach a certain number, you quit working and live happily ever after painting majestic mountain scenes or volunteering at an animal rescue center or whatever it is that makes you truly happy.

Some people hit FIRE once they've got $500,000 in the bank and plan to live on $20,000 a year for the rest of their lives under the 4 percent safe withdrawal assumption. And if that's all they need to live on, I salute them. I, however, want to have more than that stashed away, which is how Matt and I got to talking. I learned about his investments—which, when we first met, were doing better than mine—and I learned about different asset classes in real estate.

A single-family home and a duplex are two kinds of assets. With each, you're dealing with individuals, relying on information like credit scores and references from former landlords and hoping they don't steer you wrong. I was doing well for myself by owning duplexes and other residential properties, but when I started talking with Matt about how I could make the kind of money he was making, it became clear that what needed to change wasn't my strategy or even my money but my thinking. I needed to think bigger.

The kind of asset I'm now most interested in is commercial property, which means instead of renting to a person, I'm renting to UPS. Now, my biggest building is an office space. Wells Fargo is my tenant. The IRS is my tenant. I don't worry about them making rent or paying on time, and I don't worry about them calling me in the middle of the night about a broken toilet. I started playing with high-level people—people who are real hustlers worth 10 or even 100 times what I'm worth. I'm in the same room and I'm learning, for which I never forget to be grateful.

They say you're the average of the five people you spend the most time with. So, income, happiness, marriage—it's just the people you spend time with. If you spend time with people who are low net worth and who are not thinking at a high level, you're going to be the same. If you want to grow your net worth, you've got to hang around people who are millionaires. You can't be a billionaire without learning from millionaires. And you know what's amazing? Some of these guys whose bank accounts far exceed mine (at least for now) have been so generous with their time and their advice.

My friend Matt had only been doing this for a few years before we met, but he'd found a path, and when he was there, he tossed me a rope so I could find my way to the next level, too. In January 2021, I closed on my first strip mall, and now I have corporate tenants who sign long leases—and handle all the maintenance themselves.

———

My life today looks very different from my life three years ago. I'm building my business and I'm exploring what it means to be a whole, happy, healthy person. I have a beautiful wife, and in 2019, we welcomed our son Adrian. As a baby, the biggest scare he gave us was one a lot of new parents face.

He favored lying on his right side and developed a condition called plagiocephaly, which is a dramatic way of saying his head was getting a little flat. It happens to millions of kids, and the fix is simple if you catch it early enough: just encourage him to lie on the other side. We caught it a little later, and while we tried the exercises and activities to prevent it from worsening, we were not getting the correction we needed.

The skull bones fuse by a certain time, at which point there's no going back. So, we put him in a helmet designed to restrict growth in one area and allow for growth of the skull in

the other. If anything, wearing this tiny helmet just empha-
sized what a cute baby he was, and it's not something kids
need to do for years—he's not even two yet and he's already
done wearing it. It made my wife and me feel guilty, but
Adrian couldn't have been a happier, easier-to-love little boy.

My wife started to notice some changes in his growth. It
seemed like he was getting skinnier in the cheeks, and then it
seemed like he was growing more on one side of his body than
the other. But he was still on his growth curve.

He didn't have any symptoms. He didn't have a fever. He
didn't have nausea or pain. He was running around, a happy-
go-lucky kid. But my wife's maternal instincts were showing
her that something wasn't right. I'm a doctor, my family is full
of doctors, I have friends who are doctors—Adrian was
surrounded by doctors. But it was my wife who knew, when so
many people missed it, that there was a problem. She initially
thought it might be a blockage, but that didn't make sense
to me.

I look back even then on those few weeks when we
could've solved the mystery a little earlier. It wouldn't have
made much of a difference, but I wish I had been able to
somehow magically see what was going on. One day, she was
giving him a bath and pointed out the changes in his abdomen
to me. I knew we had to take it seriously.

We did a video visit with Adrian's pediatrician, who
thought it might be any number of things. As a dad and as a
doctor, my mind immediately went to a worst-case scenario—
that my precious son, so new to the world and with so much to
see and learn and do, could be sick. Really sick.

After Adrian's surgery, there were complications. A week
after the operation, when he should have been recovering and
getting ready for the next steps of his treatment, he seemed to
be getting sicker. He started vomiting green bile one day, and
his doctor realized there was an obstruction from intussuscep-

tion. Just like his cancer, it was another rare issue—so rare his surgeon had only seen it once before in his entire medical career.

Still, there were signs of hope. We weren't sure at first if his team would be able to remove the tumor in one piece. Sometimes tumors are so big or so unwieldy and matted down to other organs that all a surgeon can do is take a biopsy. If this had happened to Adrian, it would have meant a round of chemotherapy to shrink the tumor and then another operation. And the biopsy automatically upstages it to Stage Three. But we were lucky—it came out in one piece, and we learned that it had only progressed to Stage Two.

He started radiation, which can have long-term effects. When it hits a child's spine, it alters their growth. And if you just hit one side, you get scoliosis. They took steps to make sure that the curvature of his back wouldn't be affected by going across the center of the spine, but the trade-off for doing that is you end up losing a couple of inches in height.

I'm already not a tall guy! My wife is 5'4" with shoes on. Height is nothing compared to long-term health, but still, I thought, *I don't want my child to be short.* As his father, I want him to get well, and I also want to give him the best life he can possibly have. I want him to have everything and then some. After radiation came chemotherapy, which can render some kids infertile. Again, I thought, *what if my son is unable to have children of his own?* But what are any of these things, these concerns about what his future might look like, compared to his precious life, his chance to just breathe and live on earth?

———

Adrian is in the middle of his chemotherapy treatments now, and he is truly a joyful, spirited little boy. He loves playing with his trucks and climbing everything from tables to his mother, grinning at me when I take his picture. So much of what I do —everything I do—is for him, and I feel blessed that I'm able to give him a happy home and the best doctors.

I'm blessed that my financial situation is such that my wife can stay home with him and that we aren't constantly worrying about paying medical bills (although they are expensive—I opted for a high deductible health plan and HSA because I assumed we were young and healthy and would have little need for medical care. Isn't it ironic? And not in an Alanis Morissette kind of way?).

Money, though, isn't all I can give him. I think a lot of parents fall into the trap of materialism—of thinking that kids need *stuff* and it's our job to give it to them. I won't say Adrian doesn't love his toys because he does! But he also loves me, his mom and strangers he waves to when we're at Costco and that love is something he and I can give each other.

It's something I've learned from and I'm still learning from, and it was the catalyst for a lot of the personal growth work I've spent the last year doing. Because Adrian doesn't need a dad who is burned out, exhausted, stressed and angry. He needs a dad whose fire burns powerfully from within, with a flame that creates bright light, warmth and strength for him and his mom.

I won't say it's always easy or that I'm perfect because it's not and I'm not. What I will say is that the biggest lesson I've learned over the last year is that I have the power to choose happiness for myself and for my family every day. I have the power to teach my ego and rational mind to let go of what doesn't serve it and how to seek out what nourishes it. Sometimes it shocks people, but I often say that Adrian's cancer was the best thing that ever happened to me. It showed me who I am and what I'm capable of.

As I've set out on this journey, my goals are to find ways to be happier and ways to live for the now, in the now. To keep my feet solidly on the ground and my mind stretching toward the moon and beyond, because that's where I'm going.

My intentions are to dig down deep and create a solid platform from which I can keep reaching higher to realize my full human potential, to achieve financial success and to continue climbing the ladders that were set in front of me. Because I know now that I *can* go to the moon. I *can* build a real estate empire, and I *can* pursue enlightenment and inner peace at the same time.

And if I can do it? So can you.

———

Three words: intention, attention, retention.

That becomes: IN-AT-RE.

This can sound like the word "innate" (like an intrinsic part of your being) or you can add an imaginary "U" to make it sound like the word "nature."

If there is something or anything you want to accomplish, first you set the intention, like a goal.

Then you give it your attention, which means being present for the task at hand to accomplish that goal.

Finally, retention is remembering the goal and making sure it sticks with you.

You can release stress and tension by doing the above IN-AT-RE cycle. It enables you to be present and happy because you're setting and achieving goals not at random but by your own careful planning and design.

Did you know that when building a skyscraper, the height of the building is determined by the depth of its foundation? That which is built up must first be built down.

Set intentions and honor them. Dig deep and build a foundation worthy of the success that you deserve. Give yourself the gift of committing to the life you want to live, every day at every step.

FIVE

Egos and Superpowers

In Vietnam, there is a proverb that reads, "Ai giàu ba họ, ai khó ba đời" which, loosely translated, means that wealth is built and subsequently lost within three generations. The first generation is the opposite of wealthy—they're poor. They're hardworking, and that hard work is for the sole purpose of making a better life for their children and their children's children. Imagine a laborer, someone working in the fields or in a factory, putting aside a few dollars whenever they can to go toward schoolbooks, tuition or a ticket to a city or country with better opportunities.

The second generation reaps the benefits of that hard work and carries with them the memories of what it looked like. They've seen firsthand how much their parents struggled and are determined to make them proud—and to give their own children the things they went without as they worked toward a brighter tomorrow.

The third generation hears stories of the first generation, and they feel the love of the second. They, too, want to make their parents proud, maybe by going to law school or medical school or starting businesses that will eventually change the world. It's through this third generation that the dream of the first is realized—that instead of toiling for necessities, their descendants work for something greater. Something more.

What about the fourth generation? That, if you ask people who subscribe to this theory, is where wealth is lost or begins to be lost. Imagine a son taking over his father's medical practice. The son was pushed into medicine; but for his father, it was a calling. The son takes over the patient panel, but patients recognize that he is unhappy and doesn't care as much as his father did. Everyone doubts that he can maintain the family business. And then, imagine the son's son who is now lazy, playing video games all the time, apparently incapable of lifting a finger to help around the house because there's a maid and he is entitled.

Think about the stereotypical spoiled rich kid, the one who crashes his dad's Mercedes and goes to an expensive art school despite not having the drive or talent to craft great art. Or the rash of rich kids getting into car accidents while driving drunk and then using "affluenza" as a defense. The kid at the club, ordering bottle service to impress his friends with money that he didn't work for and that he doesn't deserve. The kid with the trust fund that seems like it's never going to run out—until it does.

Why does that kid spend his money on things that don't last? On things that are meant to impress other people? Why do *I* spend money on things meant to impress other people? Why do *you* do it? If owning a Ferrari, giving your wife a $100,000 Birkin bag for Christmas or buying your kid a million-dollar pony brings you joy, I'm not here to tell you that you can't have a Ferrari or a Birkin or a pony. But if you're buying Ferraris and Birkins and ponies and they don't make you feel much of anything at all, I think there's one answer to the question of why exactly you're buying them:

Ego.

If you're rolling your eyes right about now thinking, *okay, here comes another guy telling me to shed my ego and live a life of service to others*, you're not too far off base—because I am going to challenge you to do those things. I also think, though, that sometimes the concept of ego gets a bad rap.

My take on ego is that it's what helps you get work done. Your ego is where stress and pressure come from, and I don't think stress and pressure are always bad things. I had a huge ego—and I still do sometimes, which is lucky, because I have a lot of work to get done.

Ego is what pushed me to say I was going to go to Berkeley before I got in. Ego is what pushed me, once I was there, to buckle down and improve my Organic Chemistry grade. Getting a "bad" grade damaged my ego—I had an idea of myself as a smart guy who got good grades, and not living up to that was like holding a bunch of balloons and seeing one of them get popped. Medical school, as I'm sure some of you reading this are aware, is a place where egos abound, for better and for worse. We all want to impress our teachers and residents, absorb the most information, show the most promise as plastic surgeons or dermatologists or internists. That's ego!

Picture Beyoncé. Whether or not you're a fan, no one can deny her talent and her work ethic. In 2013, she directed and starred in a documentary called *Beyoncé: Life Is But a Dream*. It's a collection of material filmed over the course of her career, and in a key moment from 2011, we see Beyoncé getting ready to perform at that year's Billboard Music Awards. "Getting ready" is an understatement: the performance itself involves the human Beyoncé dancing in sync with a stage full of digital Beyoncés.

Not only do her dance moves have to be flawless, they have to match up with the clones of herself on the screens behind her. It's like matching lip-syncing to a backing track, except with her whole body and no do-overs. The rehearsals, as we see in the film, are punishing. She does the moves over

and over, willing her body to move in time with the backdrop
of perfect Beyoncés.

Later, before the show itself, Beyoncé talks into her
camcorder. It's an intimate moment with one of the world's
biggest celebrities, and she sounds exhausted. The performance she's designed might be too hard, she says. She knows
when she's bitten off more than she can chew, and she's not
too proud to admit that maybe this time things just aren't
going to go her way.

The next scene we see is the performance. It starts with no
less than Michelle Obama and Bono talking about what an
icon Beyoncé is, and features both of her parents reminiscing
about how much she wanted this very moment as a little girl.
Finally, after a countdown, Beyoncé hits the stage. Her moves
are flawless. To an observer who did not see the grit that came
before the glory, it might appear that she woke up *flawless*. She
doesn't miss a beat or a step. Seriously, you should look it up
on YouTube—but finish reading this chapter first.

Does Beyoncé have a big ego? You might say yes—she's a
huge star who jets around the world on yachts doing basically
whatever she wants whenever she wants. But I see a person
who has *balance*: the drive an ego gives you to work harder and
the humility to admit you don't have control over everything.

Beyoncé having a big ego in the harmful sense would
mean staging this expensive and elaborate show and then not
practicing at all. Saying, "I'm Beyoncé—why do I need to
rehearse when people will pay to come see me no matter
what?" When that happens, people can tell that you're missing
the mark—and why? Because you thought you were too good
to practice. Because, once again, your ego got in the way of
your success. If Beyoncé did that, she would begin to lose her
appeal and popularity, as the trust her fans placed in her to
deliver a stellar performance would begin to erode.

I'd be lying if I said that my ego has only served to help
me work harder and get smarter throughout my life, because it

hasn't. I've spent plenty of time letting my ego rule the rest of my life, and the results weren't great. I wasn't happy! And all around me, for so many years, I saw other doctors—people I was supposed to look up to—display egos so big that it's a medical miracle they were ever able to fit their heads through the doors leading to their respective operating rooms.

This shouldn't come as news to you. A lot of surgeons think they're God's gift to this earth. They think they need to have a servant or nurse follow them around everywhere and hold a little velvet plush pillow under their balls for support so that they are elevated at just the right height, perfectly cushioned, not too hot but not too cold—Goldilocks style.

The stereotype of the playboy plastic surgeon who drives an obnoxious red sports car and talks about boobs all day is a stereotype for a reason (no offense to any plastic surgeons, of course. You guys are my friends and colleagues, and we hit the interview trail together and share patients). It's doctors who let their egos take over who make it a challenge for everyone else.

They create these toxic cultures where it's okay to scream at nurses and interns and anyone who looks at them the wrong way. They steamroll patients, not thinking they need to take the time to ask questions that put people at ease. They think nobody's as smart as them. These are the people who might cut off the wrong leg in the operating room because the patient is asleep and cannot advocate for himself. These are the doctors who always think they know better than their patients.

Are people like this making the world a better place? If one of them operated on you and cured an illness that drastically improved your quality of life, you'd probably say yes. But you can perform impossible surgeries without being a jerk. In fact, not being a jerk would probably make a lot of people better doctors.

The first step in not being a jerk is realizing that you're not always right and that despite what your ego is telling you, other people know things you've never even considered. Can you with 100 percent confidence and certainty tell me that you've never made a mistake in life? That you know all the answers? Get a grip, dude. You're just one set of eyeballs, one brain, one human life that's made it to 50 years old or whatever age you are, and all you carry with you are your singular life experiences, whatever textbooks you've read and media you've consumed. And I know you, because I've been there, and I thought I knew it all. I didn't, and you don't.

You're a jerk and everyone around you can see it except for you because you don't get it. But the minute you take a chill pill and a humility pill, you'll find a lot more joy in your own life. And you'll find that people respect you more because the respect you commanded previously was not that—it was just fear. But when you are open with your heart and mind, people love you. And there's nothing on earth that can replace that feeling of infinite joy, love and bliss. There are two types of people in this world: those that get it and those who haven't gotten it yet. The ones who haven't gotten it yet will get it when they decide to open their minds and hearts.

In medical school, there are students and there are teachers. You and your classmates have spent, more or less, the same amount of time learning about medicine and what it means to be a doctor. Likewise, your teachers, more or less, are academics and working physicians who have years or even decades of experience. Once school ends, and you're thrust into residency; you're dealing with a much wider range of people—and egos.

If there are any nurses reading this book (and I hope there are), let me just say—you are amazing. Doctors can't do what they do without nurses, and a good nurse is worth more than their weight in gold. That doesn't mean that there aren't plenty of doctor versus nurse showdowns. Some of them are like sibling rivalries, but others can be stressful for everyone involved.

It starts in residency. Specifically, it starts on July 1st. Scroll through the Instagram feeds of a bunch of nurses around the end of June and you'll see the jokes. July 1st is when residents start, and some nurses like to point out how green they are—and how if you have to go to the hospital, you might want to wait until the fall. Most of them don't mean to be hurtful, but it *can* be hurtful! We've worked so hard in medical school, and we're so ready to spend the next few years working 80-hour weeks, trying to become the best doctors we can be.

At the same time, I can't imagine the feeling of being a nurse who has spent 10 or 20 years on the job and having a bunch of new doctors who don't look older than 16 come in and start telling them how to do things. I'll tell you what: the greatest doctors, surgeons and world thought leaders were, at one point, July 1st interns. I was there, too, and doctors will continue to train in this way for the foreseeable future.

Have you ever watched the TV show *Scrubs*? It does a great job of capturing the interpersonal politics and the dramas big and small that are going on in pretty much every hospital in America. There is a power dynamic: with residents, with doctors in training and nurses. There are nuances to it, and it's challenging.

When I was first starting my plastic surgery residency, I had a nurse page me. A patient was in serious pain, and she needed me to help. Again, I'd gone to medical school. I grew up around doctors. I had been preparing my whole life for this moment. And I was so afraid. I didn't know what to dose the opioid. I didn't know how to evaluate the pain. I took a long time to get back to her since I was looking it up and hemming and hawing.

I'm sure, thinking about it, that she was super upset with me! The patient was in pain, and the nurse needed me to manage the patient's pain medication. But I just didn't have the knowledge or confidence to do the right thing. I defaulted back to the check-in mentality where I ran everything by my superior and didn't think critically for myself as a doctor. I deferred blame and responsibility to my senior resident, whom I would ask for help with any little question or problem.

I recognized that fault in myself. At the end of rotation, I got a cake for the nurses, and I took that particular nurse aside.

"Hey," I said. "I remember when I started. I didn't know what I was doing, and it was wrong of me to do that."

I wasn't sure what to expect given the dynamics between residents and nurses, but her response has stuck with me to this day. She thanked me so much because no doctor had ever done that for her. It wasn't about the cake (though who doesn't love cake?). It was about me knowing that she knew better than me at that time and also about me having the humility to say, "I understand that at that time I didn't do the right thing, and I'm sorry." Years before I really started to consider what role my ego had played in my life, this was a moment where my humility and vulnerability broke through.

She was blown away and grateful for my response, which to me is a shame. Doctors and nurses spend all this time bickering and sniping behind each other's backs, but aren't we supposed to be on the same team? Why is it so hard for so many of us to put down our egos and accept that some people are going to know more than us—and that that's awesome? And to know that sometimes we're the ones who know more and to be generous with our knowledge instead of proud that we have it and someone else doesn't?

I hope you're nodding your head in recognition here—not just at my side of the story but of the nurse's. We've all been on one side or the other, and I want to challenge you: what would it look like for you to put your ego down for a minute? Seriously, I want you to know!

Think about a time in your career when you've been locked in an egocentric power struggle and do a little choose-your-own-adventure storytelling. Think about how things might have played out if the other person had been willing to put their ego aside, and then think about what would have shaken out if you'd been the one to express a little humility.

Now imagine that scenario with you and the other person as equals. As two people excited to pool their knowledge to solve a problem instead of treating it like a competition.

What would that feel like? I bet you'd feel amazing.

————

Adrian getting sick was a huge shift for me, not just in my day-to-day life but in my relationship with my own ego. The first few months of his illness were a blur, with all of us just trying to adjust to our new normal and struggling to hold it together from one day to the next. As I grappled with what he was experiencing, I felt moved to reconsider my own inner life.

In October 2020, my wife and I went on a meditation retreat. I'd begun meditating at home, and it was something I wanted to take more seriously. It was also something I wanted to share with her. I wanted us to continue to grow as a couple, to be able to relate to each other and lean on each other.

I wasn't sure what to expect. Was I going to learn all the secrets of the universe? Was I going to talk to someone from another realm? Was I going to just fall asleep?

It came through clearer than any message I've ever gotten in my entire life. As I was sitting there in a meditative state, I heard the universe speak to me. And do you want to know what it said?

"You don't know shit."

The universe, in its infinite wisdom, had looked deep into my soul and figured out that what I needed was permission to acknowledge that I don't, in fact, know anything. To embrace it. To put my ego down, stop feeling pressure to be in control of everything all the time and just…*be*.

When I went back to work, my office staff noticed that

something was different about me. "You're being uncharacter-istically nice today," they said. "What happened?"

Not feeling quite ready to process my experience with anyone besides my closest circle, I attributed the new, chill Dr. Patrick Tran to the fact that I had just gotten a new car, a beautiful white Tesla Model X with white interior and these cool falcon-wing doors that catch people's eyes when I'm cruising around in Modesto. And yes, the non-Alanis Morrissette irony of me starting this chapter with an exhortation to reconsider why we get so excited about new cars and then telling people that getting a new car changed my life is not lost on me.

A few months later, we were lucky enough to be able to attend a second retreat, this one over the course of two nights. Part of me had wondered if maybe what I'd experienced was a one-off, but during my second retreat, I had similar insights and feelings.

The second day, we were getting a meditation inner circle, and I was incredibly deep into my journey. Other people in the room were sitting down and meditating, and I was lying facedown on a mattress. I remember hearing everything: the guru leading the meditation and everyone's lungs breathing together in beautiful synchrony.

But I was in a different world. I was the most ecstatic, most blissful, most at peace I had ever been in my entire life just lying down, feeling everyone's energy together as if we were not separate but one single organism. As if my ego, which has served me in so many ways and continues to do so, was gently floating away, unburdening me from having to carry it around all the time.

With every breath, I felt my body lifting like I was floating on a fluffy cloud. I didn't even know that such happiness existed until then. Imagine infinite joy, love and bliss simultaneously, all while recognizing the oneness of everything. I'm not sure I can put it on paper. It's like trying to describe sex to a virgin. You can only say so much about it in words, but until you've experienced the divine, you won't get it. Going to this retreat helped me access this state of mind, but it's one I've been able to keep tapping into on my own.

There are many ways that people throughout the world and in history have managed to get to that sense of peace and bliss, whether it's Zen Buddhism, meditation, yoga, church, sacred medicines, quiet contemplation on your own—whatever works best for you is the thing that works best for you. Some people devote their entire lives to it, but you don't have to. None of us do. We just have to be willing and open to the idea that inner peace isn't a punchline to a corny joke, and it's not something we'll never achieve. We have to consider putting down our egos and reveling in the freedom that comes next.

Despite feeling like my eyes had been opened after a lifetime of not seeing what was directly in front of me, I'm still myself. I still have an ego, and I still struggle to find the balance between using it to power my drive and letting it drive me.

For example, take this book you're currently reading. It didn't spring from my head fully formed—I had to work on it, and work on it a lot. I don't exactly have a lot of free time these days between Adrian and my family and my work and my investments and the occasional late-afternoon hot tub soak that is a crucial part of my self-care. I spend a lot of time on the phone with mentors and mentees, clients, patients and people I want to learn from.

I spend so much time on the phone that my wife, as I was writing this very chapter, put her foot down. She was tired of watching me do 10 things at once and tired of talking to me only to discover that I was also talking to someone else via my headphones. Her solution was simple—she gave me set hours that, no matter what else is going on, I am not on the phone and not working on anything besides loving my family (which is the opposite of work).

There were two paths for me here. I could let my ego do the talking and insist that I can do it all, all the time. Or I could look at myself and my schedule and be humble. Acknowledge that I've been taking on a lot of projects and that juggling them all is going to take occasionally putting something aside for a few hours.

I chose option two. I told the people I work with and talk to most often that during these hours on these days, I'm not available—not to expect texts from me, emails from me or calls from me. This doesn't cost me a thing, though an earlier version of me might have worried about missing out on something important. What I'm getting is way more valuable than what I'm giving up, and I can't wait for the weekend, when I get to spend blissful mornings in the company of the two people I love most in the world.

How could my ego compete with that?

———

Someone I admire a lot is a man named Ram Dass. Born Richard Alpert, he wasn't much for religion or mysticism or spirituality. He studied psychology and eventually became a tenured professor at Harvard. Not a bad gig!

In the 1960s, he traveled to India and his whole life changed. He devoted himself to the study of Hinduism and eventually wrote *Be Here Now*, largely considered the first text meant to help non-Hindus learn about the religion. For decades, he gave away all the royalties that came from the book's sales and worked to share what he'd learned not as a traditional teacher but as a fellow seeker.

In 1997, he had a stroke that left him, for the first time in his life, completely dependent on the care of others. He chose to interpret the stroke and his subsequent need for round-the-clock care not as a punishment but as a gift, a message from the universe to go inward and deeper. He had devoted his life to learning and teaching and now, in his 60s, he was understanding for the first time what it felt like to really need other people. "I would not wish you the stroke," he says, "but I do wish you the grace that came from it."

That's why I say Adrian getting sick has been one of the best things that ever happened to me.

If you had asked me five years ago what my superpower was, I might have talked about my doctoring skills or my money. I might not have been able to answer the question without making a joke. Aren't superpowers for kids?

I know now that I have a superpower. My superpower, the one that unveiled itself—or as my wife, Modesto's number-one *RuPaul's Drag Race* superfan, might put it, "RU-VEALED" itself—when my son got sick and I had to look beyond my ego, is this:

I have the power to find the grace in every moment. To find the beauty in how life unfolds.

It's a blessing, and it feels like an even bigger blessing to be able to say, with 100 percent certainty, that *everyone* has a superpower. If you're reading this? You have a superpower, and it has nothing to do with your work or your bank account or your car, even if you are literally Batman and your car is the Batmobile.

It's there, waiting for you to unlock it. From there, the possibilities are endless.

———

I'm writing this book in the summer of 2021, a period when most of the world has been wearing face coverings for the last 18 months in an attempt to stop the spread of the COVID-19 pandemic. As vaccines have rolled out, it has become possible for us, in some situations, to take our masks off and regain some semblance of normalcy. Never before have so many people felt so collectively grateful for the feeling of fresh air moving unobstructed through our noses, or the warmth of the sun on our entire faces.

What if ego functions the same way as an N95 mask? Protecting us when we need it to, but slowing us down and making it feel harder to breathe when we don't need it to? Think about when you can choose to put your ego down and experience the miracle of an unobstructed breath of fresh air. How about we take off our ego masks?

Choose humility, and let it guide you to the grace that exists within struggle.

SIX

Mindset Over Matter

Have you ever tried to update your iPhone software to the latest and greatest, but you're using an old phone from six generations ago? You know how it is—a new operating system comes out and promises clearer photos, faster apps and thousands of new emojis to text with. But then you get a telltale message: the new software is incompatible with your old hardware.

That's the best way I can describe the role mindset plays in my life and probably in yours, too. If you're stuck in a space of "why me," a space of envy, a space of assuming every resource is finite, then I promise you that no amount of money or success is going to bring you happiness. If your mindset isn't one of abundance, then more money just means more expenditures. Generally, you will maintain your unhealthy habits of unconscious spending and end up with more problems. How is it possible for you to be giving when you are constantly worried that you will run out of money or any other resource at any given time?

The reason that toilet paper went on back order during the COVID-19 pandemic is a scarcity mindset. People went out and bought toilet paper as if they were stuck in a blizzard. As if it wasn't a respiratory illness going around, but one that causes massive and incessant diarrhea for everyone. And toilet paper manufacturers could not keep up. They generally make enough for everyone at any given time, but they couldn't suddenly ramp up production and kill 10 million trees in a day because of a public freak-out.

A scarcity mindset means a version of yourself continuously trying to upgrade your software when what you really need is new hardware. While you can't swap or physically upgrade your brain (yet!), you *can* choose to live in an abundant world. You *can* choose to live in a friendly universe, one in which everything goes your way. You *can* live your life in a space where you are enough, you are worthy, you are generous. Where every resource is infinite. Where you are infinite. And when you choose to live this way, you will be amazed at what magical transformations occur in your life.

When you shift to an abundance mindset, you upgrade your mental hardware, like getting the latest and greatest computer chip that is way faster and more powerful. You can't replace your brain, but you can replace your negative attitude with positive thoughts. You can replace your poor mindset with a wealthy mindset. Then, the entire mental operating system is upgraded. You go from You 1.X to You 2.0. You remove the invisible walls of the sandbox in which you were playing before, that tiny arena where you felt safe and protected but also the one in which you couldn't accomplish anything of substance and were at risk of contracting worms from the cats pooping in it while you were not paying attention.

Now, you scale over the little walls of the barrel and no other crab can claw you back down. Now, you go beyond your limitations and journey into the infinitely expansive universe of which you are an integral part. Now, you recognize and remember who you really are and where you came from. Now, you know that you're an infinite being in a physical form. You realize that even your human body is a sandbox, and your soul and awareness and consciousness are deeper, wider, longer, bigger and more expansive. You become limitless and can navigate the universe with grace.

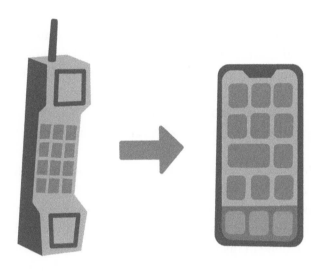

There's no manual on how to feel when your son has cancer. There's no course in medical school that teaches you how to take care of your own family when they have a serious illness.

People come to me for healing when I'm dying on the inside, worrying about my son. I put on a brave face at work. I'm friendly to my patients, and many of them don't have a clue that my son is at home fighting for his life.

And then I think: I have it hard? My son just barely turned two years old. He doesn't deserve this. He doesn't deserve to get freaked out going to the hospital and not understanding what's going on. He doesn't deserve to have had two surgeries when other kids his age are happily running around and playing with their friends. He doesn't deserve to have chemotherapy and radiation—which is hard enough on an adult, let alone a little boy small enough for me to hold in my arms.

He doesn't deserve to lose his thick, curly hair from chemotherapy. He doesn't deserve to have a feeding tube shoved down his nostril into his stomach because he can't keep food down from the chemo. He doesn't deserve to have his immune system wiped out every three or four weeks so that he can't fight an infection, meaning he's in the hospital when he has a simple fever in addition to getting chemotherapy treatments that make fevers so dangerous in the first place.

He doesn't deserve the chance that he could die before me, his dad.

So, if Adrian doesn't deserve what's happening to him, I had to wonder: is it something I did? Are all the bad things that I've done in my life coming back to haunt me? Is it all the bad karma that I've ever created? Every person I've hurt? Was it the doctor's fault? Did the doctor miss it at his last physical, when he pushed on his belly and said, "No tumor, no masses, everything's fine," even though my wife was concerned about his weight?

Who is going to step up and take responsibility for this cancer? My mind went to some unhealthy places. I'm a doctor: I know, objectively and on paper, that there's nothing that my wife or I did that made Adrian get sick. But that doesn't mean I didn't wonder. I would lie awake at night and drive myself crazy thinking about all the mistakes I've made, all the people I've treated badly over the course of my life.

I've done some things I'm not proud of, and I felt, in my darkest moments, like maybe Adrian's cancer was a punishment the universe had sent me. Like maybe all the people who think I'm an asshole sent this energy into the world, and it manifested in the form of my sweet little boy getting sick.

You know who that was, whispering those things in my ear? My ego.

Remember when I said that the greatest gift meditation gave me was the freedom to acknowledge that I don't know shit? I had to tap into that insight to push beyond the idea that Adrian's sickness had anything to do with me. I wouldn't wish what he and our family are going through on my worst enemy. And I have to believe that if you asked every single person I've ever wronged if they'd be glad we're in this place, they'd say no.

I was so angry, and I had to come to a place of realizing that my anger and my ego weren't serving me. All those thoughts that I let fester and the stories I told myself were not helping. *They did not make things better.* In fact, they made things worse! Because they took root in my brain like weeds in a beautiful garden and kept me in a space of feeling self-centered. A space of victimhood. It made me powerless, and most importantly, it didn't help Adrian. Because when my mindset wasn't right, I did not have the capacity and the strength to help him.

It was just like dying inside, being eaten alive by stress and fear and worry when I needed to be a source of strength and positive energy for my son. It wasn't until I made the conscious decision and effort to say to myself, *Adrian has cancer and aside from what I'm already doing, there's nothing I can do about it.* And to ask myself: what choices am I going to make now? What stories am I going to tell myself now? How am I going to shift my mindset so that instead of waking up every day worrying about what's going to happen, I wake up every day feeling at peace with the knowledge that "What is going to happen today?" is a question I'll never actually be able to answer.

It's only then that I could focus on the positive thoughts

and bring them into Adrian's life. Because you can't give what
you don't have. It wasn't until I took responsibility for every
aspect of my life that I found my way back to happiness. Now,
instead of bringing Adrian grief, sorrow and pain, I bring him
joy, hope and love.

When I found grace and beauty in the worst moments of
my life, those moments ceased to be the worst moments of my
life. When your mind is closed, when you're so wrapped up in
yourself that you aren't making space for light to shine
through the cracks of whatever darkness you've found yourself
mired in, then you're closing off your perception, judgment
and ability to make good decisions. Most importantly, you're
closing yourself off to possibility.

Learning to genuinely open my mind this way was a
turning point. I realized that I take 100 percent responsibility
for what happens to Adrian. I *can* take ownership for turning
every dial, pushing every button and adjusting every slider
that is in my reach in the battle against this cancer.

I'm an ultimate fighter, and I have moved past the point of
rules. I am kicking ass and taking names. I'm not pulling any
punches, and I will bite, claw, elbow, headbutt, pile drive, curb
stomp, pull hair, gouge eyes, sweep the leg, go for the jugular,
kick it when it's down and spit in its face at the end of a truly
no-holds-barred competition of me versus CCSK. I *will* fight
for his life harder than anything I've ever fought for.

Adrian's a brave little toaster too and he's in the ring with
me, along with Alicia. I don't carry one iota of doubt in my
mind that we will be victorious when the bell rings. Every fiber
in my being knows that our family will come out of this
stronger than ever. I don't mean that through the sheer force
of will I'm going to cure Adrian's cancer, and I don't mean
that any parent who has a child facing cancer just isn't trying
hard enough to get their kids well. What I mean is: why not?

Why wouldn't Adrian get better? He's already survived so
much, and he's already been so lucky. How amazing is it that

I'm a doctor and my family is filled with doctors, so we're able to understand his treatment plans at every step of the way? How amazing is it that Adrian's surgeon was skilled enough to remove his tumor in one go? How amazing is it that we live in a time and place where radiation and chemotherapy are readily available and have been proven to work on cancers like Adrian's and in children as young as he is?

Adrian's life is a miracle. It's a gift. Once I opened my eyes to that magic, it became easy for me to approach each day not with dread but with gratitude. To shift my mindset from "What did I do to deserve this terrible thing?" to "My son, my wife and I deserve to be happy, healthy and full of love and joy, so that's what we're going to be."

My wife Alicia recently told me that while she was in the hospital with Adrian, she went downstairs to grab some dinner in the cafeteria. As she walked to the elevator, she noticed a woman bawling her eyes out, literally on the floor with a phone held to her ear and sobbing a cry that only a broken spirit can create from the vocal cords.

Astoundingly, Alicia told me that people were walking by this poor woman without stopping! My beautiful guardian angel of a wife went over and put her arm around the lady. I'm not sure what possesses your average human being to walk by a soul that is crying for help like that, but I'm glad that Alicia stopped to help. The woman was destroyed because her four-year-old daughter had just died in the pediatric ICU.

The woman was crying on the floor of a hospital and people were just walking past her, stepping over her and trying to not make eye contact. I cried when my wife told me this. Not only for the woman's grief over her dead daughter but also for the lack of human compassion demonstrated by whatever doctors, nurses, patients or whoever else ignored her.

I am so grateful that my wife was there to put her arm around the woman and say, "Hey, you are right here. Touch the floor with your hand. Wiggle your toes. Come back into your body—you're right here, right now." Alicia gave the woman her number, and she texted her thank you right away.

I cannot imagine the depth of pain felt by that woman and am so glad that my wife was able to bring her a modicum of comfort in a time of despair. I cannot fathom how I would feel if Adrian were to pass. And I know that if I were bawling my eyes out, rolling on the hospital floor, I'd appreciate it if you, my reader, would stop by for a minute and say, "Hey, it's okay. Take a breath. Open your eyes. Come back to earth."

And I pray that the next time you walk past anyone in distress, you look up from your electronic device, wake up from your dazed slumber and actually see another human being that is not physically you but who really *is* you, who really needs help, and you take a moment out of your schedule to help them.

———

Billionaires—the ones who didn't inherit their money—don't begin by saying "I want to put money in my pocket." They begin by identifying a problem and developing a novel solution. That's where the money comes from—not from greed or desire but from *service*.

When you come to work from a place of service, where you're thinking about the wants and needs of someone other than you, it sticks. Now, I'm not naïve: I don't think Jeff Bezos and Elon Musk are humble guys who just wanted to be of service to their fellow man. The goal of Amazon isn't *not* to make money. But why do people like Amazon? Because it works. Because when you need something fast and at the best price, it's there. The people who start companies like that can open their eyes and minds and look at the big picture, and I truly believe that kind of abundance mindset is available to everyone.

A few years ago, I was taking a course on investing in real

estate geared toward doctors. Another student got up to share her story. I'll never forget it. She was working in a free clinic, and for context, as a private practice physician in a high-demand specialty, I earned four times her salary—even though I'm not an owner of a company and I take a W2.

She shared that within one year, her real estate portfolio became massive. There's no other way to put it: she was crushing it. She started with one home—a single-family home. It was a safe bet, and then she got a taste for the game. Then she got bigger and bigger until her portfolio dwarfed that of many other doctors.

It would have been easy for me to look at her and think, *What does she know that I don't? Is she smarter than me? Is she luckier than me?*

But that's subsistence, not abundance. That's a mindset where you think everything is finite and that you're always, always in competition for every resource. The wrong kind of thinking that one person having an awesome portfolio means your portfolio is either going to be less awesome or more awesome, when in reality, I believe there are enough opportunities for all of us to crush it. Instead of coveting what she had, I chose to believe I could have those things, too—not by taking them away from someone else but by doing the work and earning my own version of that success.

With that abundance mindset, with claiming an identity of wealth, with taking ownership of every outcome in my life, I now command a real estate portfolio worth, at the time of this writing, more than $22,000,000.

I didn't get there by shaking out the couch cushions for loose change and stashing it away in my piggy bank. I readily admit, as you now know, that I've been very privileged and that I consider myself lucky to earn the kind of money that I earn. But I worked to get where I am, and as much as I feel lucky, I also feel proud of myself. I feel proud that I can take my salary and invest it and turn it into something even bigger for my family. And I have the humility to acknowledge that I made some lucky bets that paid off handsomely.

Really, I could stop there. I could stop at believing that positivity flows and will flow from the universe and into my life and into the lives of people that I love. I don't think anyone would find fault with that.

But I want to go further. An abundance mindset, for me, means that what's available to me is available to everyone. The lessons I've learned about letting go of my ego and choosing love and happiness are important lessons that have absolutely changed my life for the better. So why should I want to keep them to myself?

Once upon a time, I was standing in my own way. I was so selfish, and I didn't see the big picture. I was chasing things that weren't worth chasing. Now, I'm chasing meaning. I'm chasing peace and positivity. I'm creating abundance, and I know now that true abundance is taking what you have and sharing it with other people. I know that in sharing my journey to practice humility, I'm encouraging other people to embrace humility in their own lives, and it's there that I've been blessed with a path forward.

———

You can make money flipping couches. Seriously: you can go out to the street on trash day, when people leave their unwanted furniture at the curb, and you can pick up a couch for free, clean it and reupholster it and then sell it on Facebook Marketplace or Craigslist or to one of your friends. There are so many hustles, whether you want to pick up lucrative side work in medicine or start an Etsy shop selling embroidered art your grandma makes. You might not make the kind of money you'll make investing in real estate, but you will make some.

The idea that you can make money doing pretty much anything isn't something a lot of people will tell you, largely because there are a lot of people making money telling you their way is the only way or the best way. I know a lot about real estate investing, and I believe it's a great option for doctors who want to take their salaries and leverage them into big money, so that's why it's the strategy I focus on in this book (and if you're wondering, "Patrick, when are we going to get to the details?" they're coming!).

You can lose your shirt in real estate, too. The cycle of boom-and-bust repeats itself every so often. The market could crash like it did in 2008. Or you could make the wrong choice of property manager. Or you could have the bad luck to buy a bunch of duplexes on a street that gets hit with a freak tornado for which you did not purchase insurance.

This is where the difference between being rich and being wealthy comes into play for me. Being rich is simple—it means you have a lot of money. People quibble on exactly how much money you need to have to be officially rich, but if you pull up your bank statements and the numbers you see match your idea of rich, you're rich. Wealth, on the other hand, is more complicated.

I think of myself as wealthy not just because I have money but also because I have a family. I have friends, I have passions, I have dreams. I have, at the end of the day, a mindset that helps me believe in my own wealth no matter what. That you could take away all the zeroes in my bank account, but you cannot take away my skill set and abilities, so I would hustle and make it all back and more. That mindset also means I feel a responsibility to be a good person—as good a person as I can be. I feel a responsibility to treat people well.

When I have a patient, whether they're new or they've seen me a hundred times, I have to generate rapport as soon as I walk into the room. The surgery I specialize in involves cutting people's faces, which requires a not-small amount of trust. The patient might be 90 years old—somebody's mom, somebody's grandmother. Maybe their daughter is in the room, too, and I have to walk in there and find a way to communicate:

> Hey, I'm going to take care of you. You can trust me. I'm here to help you. I'm here to take all my training and all my expertise—all the textbooks I've read, surgeries I've done, patients I've served and my cumulative life experience—and turn that knowledge into a concrete result that will make your life better. The collective energy and ability of the entire universe from my ancestors' DNA passed down to me is all in my hands now, and I'm going to channel that wisdom and deliver it to you.

That's no easy feat, as I'm sure many of you are aware.

People can read about me before they come in. They can look at my biography on my website, check reviews or ask around. But at the end of the day, these people don't know me. We're in the room together, and while I'm the doctor, we're both just people.

You can have all the credentials in the world and still be a jerk. As a physician, part of my job is to have a great bedside manner, to instantly make my patients feel safe with me. When you walk into a doctor's office, you know you're going to see a surgeon, but if you met me at Costco, you wouldn't necessarily think, "I definitely want to let this guy near my face with a knife." Not because I don't seem perfectly nice when I'm shopping at Costco, but because it's not human nature to trust strangers in that way.

A healthy mindset, to me, makes thinking of patient interactions like this as a gift. Instead of creating an adversarial relationship where it's my job to talk at them and it's their job to listen to me because I'm the expert, I can honor the fact that they are putting all their trust and their hopes for healing in my hands. That they, too, are trying to remember to put their egos down.

———

If you took away all my material possessions today, even if I went bankrupt, I would not be fazed. I know that I could get it back. I would get it back quicker than how I built it up to begin with. That's something no one can take away—my mindset. Your mindset is something no one will be able to take away from you.

It's the most valuable thing in the world that also happens to be totally free.

———

I had some trouble with the refrigerator at my new house, so I called my handyman to check it out. He discovered, after pulling it out from its spot in the kitchen, that a rat had found its way into the walls or crevices of the house and chewed at one of the hoses, because chewing at hoses is what rats do and the refrigerator seemed like a good source of water, which rats, like all living beings on earth, need to survive.

A lot of people who are focused on making as much money as possible —no matter what, no matter where the money comes from—are like the rat. They leave trails of destruction (or in the case of my house, a single chewed-up water hose) in their wake, so singularly focused on money that they're blind to anyone or anything that stands in their way. The problem with a rat chewing through the hose is that once air is in the line, water stops running. The well runs dry, and now you need another place to source your water. It would have made much more sense for the rat to find a way to get the water from a renewable source.

Rats are incredibly smart creatures, capable of accessing water in even the driest of places, but they also have short lifespans. They get into accidents, they get into fights, they get, in the case of the rat in my house, captured in traps where they die. However much water they might have gotten yesterday ceases to matter.

What if instead of being like the rat in search of water, we imagined ourselves as people walking through the desert? Sure, it's hot and sandy. But in addition to water, there's something else all living beings need: air. And air, in the desert, is plentiful.

There's no end to the air people can breathe in the desert, and it's a self-renewing resource. You can stand next to someone in the desert and breathe all the air that you want, and guess what? It doesn't suck the air out from their breath. They can live and enjoy the warm breeze, too! What if we thought of money as air? It's all around us, just waiting for us to take a deep breath in. There exists enough money in the world to feed every mouth and provide clean drinking water to every human. It's just shifted into deep pockets or concentrated heavily in some areas more than others.

So, if there's more than enough money in the world, and money can be created out of thin air, then it becomes a matter of creating and shifting it for you. And also remembering to contribute and give to others who are not as blessed or lucky as yourself. The beauty of thinking this way is that there's enough air for everyone to have as much as they need. The same goes for money.

Live in abundance—not just for yourself but for the people around you. Then, see how positive energy spreads.

SEVEN

The Meaning of Wealth

I know plenty of people who make more money than me and who are worth more money than me. I do well enough, but I'm not Jeff Bezos.

More importantly, I don't *want* to be Jeff Bezos. He went to space, sure, but how much time does the guy get to spend with his family? To just...take an afternoon off to hang out because the weather is nice? I'm not here to judge, but I wonder: how many happy marriages end in divorce?

I have money, but I also have love. I have a beautiful family, and their love for me is a shining light, a beacon on even the worst days, reminding me that the three of us are in this together no matter what. Since Adrian was diagnosed, I've also been lucky to have the love and support of my extended family—his illness has, in many ways, brought us even closer as we all direct our energy toward healing him.

What I have, in short, is *wealth*. I want you to be wealthy, too. Part of wealth is financial security and independence, but that's not the only pillar holding up the temple that is your body and soul. In thinking about how best to describe what I think wealth is and how I think you accumulate it, I came up with an acronym.

Are you ready?

WEALTH.

Each of these letters represents a different aspect of wealth, so without further ado, I'm going to break it down for you.

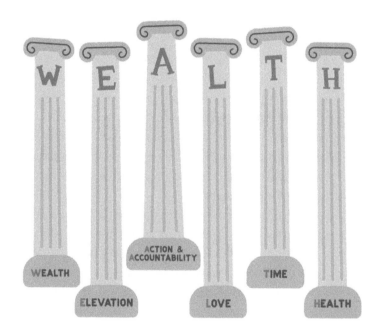

W Stands for Wealth

It's more than the number of zeroes in your bank account. Those zeroes aren't just there to give you a thrill every time your face unlocks your iPhone and you see your balances on your handheld screen (I won't judge you if it *does* give you a thrill, though).

You are still you, no matter the number of zeroes in your bank account.

Seriously: when is the last time you thought about the point of money? As kids, some of us probably imagined growing up and driving Ferraris and living in beachside mansions that also doubled as superhero headquarters. I remember riding a jet ski for the first time at five years old, and I loved the feeling of the waves, the vibration of the engine transferring to my little hands. That feeling stuck with me for the next 30-ish years, and with it came the dream to buy my very own jet ski.

I can afford it, but I still haven't taken myself down to the store to realize five-year-old Patrick's dream. Once you hit a certain age or certain life milestones, even being rich feels a lot less sexy. I love trips to the Apple Store to shop for new gadgets as much as the next guy, but you know what else I love? Knowing that if my hot water heater craps out tomorrow, I can afford to buy a new one and have it installed without having to think twice.

In a more urgent sense, I love the peace of mind that comes with knowing that Adrian's treatment isn't going to bankrupt our family and that my wife can stay home with him and not have to worry about pinching pennies.

That jet ski dream was not simply limited to the ownership of the vehicle, but it was a grander vision. Not only the jet ski but also the freedom to enjoy it at my convenience. To ride the waves of the ocean at a moment's notice. The smell of the salty ocean air, the sound of the seagulls flying by, the warmth of the sand beneath my toes. The beautiful home right on the waterfront, where after a morning spent exploring the ocean, I sit down to fresh ceviche and homemade tortilla chips with the most delectable guacamole you've ever tasted, made by my beautiful wife for our family.

Money gives you opportunity and lets you capitalize on other things that magnify who you are. If you're a generous person, genuinely interested in the lives of other people, then money gives you the chance to help in a material way. If you're a doctor working in private practice or in a large hospital system, a massive increase in wealth might mean cutting back on time spent on call for your patients so you can spend more time at home with your wife and son who are so excited when you walk through the door each night.

It might mean quitting your corporate medical job where you're treated like a commodity instead of a person and working at a free clinic for low or no pay, because you're financially free and now are able to afford prioritizing your values and filling not only your wallet but also your soul.

Money can fix a lot of low-level problems so that you can deal with high-level stuff. It's like Maslow's Hierarchy of

Needs: when you're hungry, it's very challenging to repair a mindset stuck in an unhealthy place.

If you don't have a place to live, then you're probably not able to spend a lot of time thinking about ego. Money isn't going to get you to the top of the pyramid; you can't buy your way to inner peace. You can provide for your family, though. You can give to causes close to your heart, and you can outsource the things you hate so you can spend more time doing the things you love.

You can also do these things from the deck of your new beach house, soaking in the most vibrant sunset you've ever had the privilege to witness.

E Stands for Elevation

This is you leveling up, not just financially but in every aspect of your life. You're elevating your state. You're elevating your mindset. Let's say you're climbing a mountain: you've made it to the next stop, and someone throws you a rope you can use to climb higher. Then, because elevation is also about elevating other people, you throw that rope down to someone who hasn't made it as far as you have yet.

You hang out with a tribe of people who push you and cheer you on—they want you to keep climbing that mountain because they know you can do it and because they know how sweet it will be when you're all at the summit together.

Think about the people in your life—your family, your friends, your coworkers. Do you want to climb a mountain with them? Do they make you feel like you can do it?

As I mentioned earlier, there's a concept that you're the average of the five people you spend the most time with. This is true across socioeconomic status, race, weight, religion—you name it, and it applies. If all your friends weigh 600 pounds, then you're probably okay being heavier than what would be a healthy or ideal body weight for you. If your friends are all poor, you may feel good about being slightly less poor.

It's the same thing that we talked about in the chapter on

mindset. Elevating your mindset happens first within, and then you turn it outward: who can you elevate? Who are you looking to for guidance, for advice? Elevation means that you're being pushed outside your comfort zone. That you're stretching and growing. Brooke Castillo says, "Discomfort is the currency of your dreams." Learning to sit with discomfort when you decide to step up in your life, learning to choose progress over perfection and to turn your adversity into an advantage—this is the first thing you must do if you're going to fly to the moon.

A Stands for Action + Accountability

The only reason that I get to do what I do is because I take massive action. If you have a wealth and abundance of action and activity, you'll get a lot done. It's easy to not take action. It's easier than doing literally anything else, and it's designed that way! Taking action is a muscle you have to exercise. No one wakes up one day and says, "You know what? Today I think I'm going to change my whole life" and then actually finds their whole life changed by bedtime.

Here's a mini-challenge I want you to do:

What's something you've been putting off? If you're saying to me, "Patrick, there's nothing I've been putting off because I never procrastinate!" I'll know you're lying.

Pick one thing from the list and do it. Just one! It doesn't have to be a big task—it can be tiny! Instead of washing the whole sink full of dishes, just decide you'll wash one dish and call that a win.

Every night, set an alarm on your phone to wash one dish at 8 pm after you've had dinner and before you're too tired. If you wash that one dish successfully, call it a win. Make it a chain, like Jerry Seinfeld recommends for novice comedians. Write a joke every day, mark the date with a red slash on the calendar, then don't break the streak. So for you, maybe that's washing a dish every day. Or reading one page in a textbook every day. Or writing 100 words for your book every day. Then, you put the list away and come back to it the next day when you'll pick one more thing. Really feel it in your mind and body. What does it feel like to do the thing? What does it feel like to be *done* with it?

The beauty of this technique is that you give yourself permission to start, but you can also count your wins. If you wash just one dish, you can feel the win and it will help you maintain a consistent habit even when you're tired or not feeling well. And if you complete the whole sink full of dishes, that's a win, too!

I learned this concept from a scene shared by the monk Ajahn Brahm in his book *Opening the Door of Your Heart*. The story, which I will paraphrase, follows a famous abbot building a new hall in his monastery that unfortunately has to be stopped mid-construction when heavy rains come. A visitor sees the half-finished building days later and asks when it will be finished. The old monk replies, "The hall is finished." The visitor is incredulous, his eyeballs practically dangling from their sockets at this response. "What do you mean the hall is finished?" the visitor exclaims. "There's no roof! There's construction debris all over the place!" The old abbot gently smiles and replies, "What's done is finished," and goes on his merry way to meditate.

My take-home message is this: the work in your life will never be finished. You will constantly have more to do. Dirty dishes will always accumulate in the sink because you will always have to eat. At some point, you've got to call it a day and acknowledge the work that you have done. You stop, smell the roses and enjoy some relaxation. You can't work forever. The lesson is that you take small, actionable steps but also prevent yourself from burning out. Because without rest, there can be neither sustainable nor massive action taken.

On accountability, there's a quote by Rumi, the 13th-century Persian poet, that I want to share:

"Set your life on fire. Seek those who fan your flames."

In other words, seek the people who add kindling to the fire inside of you. The person who has the most power to do that? It's you. It's the version of you that has flexed the "taking action" muscle so many times that taking action isn't something you have to struggle with any longer.

You'll get there. And until then, I'll be right alongside you, fanning your flames.

Accountability, to me, means living a life filled with people who aren't afraid to hold a mirror up to your face when you aren't looking your best. Not in a nasty, mean or judgmental way, criticizing you for your lack of sleep or your makeup but in an open, constructive and honest way.

Maybe someone is losing his mind at the airport, taking it out on the flight attendants, and you're ready to punch him in the face—but your wife reminds you, "Remember, we don't know what he's going through. He could be stressed about catching a flight to see a sick parent or his dying child. Let's extend him some grace in this moment."

Or you're being a jerk to your staff, and your colleague simply tells you, "Hey, maybe don't do that." When I'm trying to solve a problem the wrong way, or ignoring a problem that needs my attention, my life coach is there. I can call him to work on any problem.

If I have a challenge with my real estate investments, my high-level peer group will get real with me: "Dude, this is a dumpster fire if you don't fill that vacancy." It lights a fire under my ass, which serves two purposes: first, it helps me take care of my own side of the street. Second, it gives me the motivation to help my friends when they're the ones who have blind spots and need an authentic look in the mirror.

L Stands for Love

This pillar of wealth is very straightforward. You *need* love in your life. Whatever that means to you! If you're married, love your partner and let them love you in return. Learn to love them in the way that they receive it best and ask them to love you in the way you receive it best. Fill each other's love tanks, a term that comes from *The Five Love Languages* by Gary Chapman. If you're single, then love your friends and family and allow them to love you in return. Love, like action, is a muscle: the more you practice, the stronger it becomes.

Loving someone means being vulnerable, and I understand how scary that is. Without the sparks of love, though, your fire is going to burn out. I'm also not saying it's always easy! Loving Adrian, for example, is the easiest thing in the world. In addition to being my son, he's also an incredibly cute kid. And I know everyone thinks their kid is the cutest, but objectively my kid is the cutest, and I would challenge anyone to look into his shining eyes or hear his infectious laugh and not feel the love energy he radiates from his beautiful soul.

Other relationships require a little more effort. More time, more compromise, more of everything that can fall by the wayside when you're in a competitive and cutthroat residency program and your only goal is to come out ahead of your cohort, for example.

It can feel even harder to love someone or something that is hard to love. Compassion comes from cultivating this though. Maybe you are having a tough time loving someone who has wronged you. Someone who is a stranger to you. Someone whose values and actions don't align with yours. But for your own joy and peace, you will find that you must learn to love them anyway.

You know who you really have to love, though?

Yourself.

You can dismiss that as woo-woo nonsense all you want, but might I remind you that none other than the great RuPaul "Mama Ru" Charles agrees! Every time this iconic drag queen superstar legend reminds us of the essential truth: "If you can't love yourself, how in the hell are you going to love somebody else? Can I get an amen up in hurrr okurrrr?!?!" we say, "Yaaas queen! Slay all day!" And by "we," I mean my wife and I because we've never missed an episode of *Drag Race*. My wife Alicia loves to watch the show, and I love my wife Alicia; therefore, I watch shows that she watches, and she, in turn, lets me drag her to ride roller coasters and do things that I enjoy more than she does.

Part of loving yourself, to me, is embracing the fact that you deserve every good thing you want. That every person in your life, every ad and every message that told you that you're not worthy or good enough was wrong. As we grow up from childhood, we often shift from living in a constant state of joy and wonder to one of victimhood. This happens through the negative interactions we experience in life, from bullying and indoctrination into broken school systems to advertising that tells us that we're nothing without a Rolex or Porsche (which is criminal, because we all know that when the excitement fades from that new shiny object we bought, we end up back where we were to begin with).

There's nothing wrong with choosing to wear makeup or getting Botox or liposuction or a face-lift. The problem arises when we believe that these things will solve all the unrelated problems in our lives. Anyone who works in plastic surgery or dermatology has seen the kind of patient who comes in thinking, "This breast augmentation (or laser or filler injection) is going to be the thing that finally makes me happy." They're looking for it to stop a divorce or gain a promotion. While they may have their cheeks fuller with beautiful volume restoration or more radiant skin after laser energy, they remain unhappy. Because regardless of any external change, their internal state is the same.

You deserve to live a life filled with financial security and action with people who hold you accountable and who love you just for being you, regardless of what you look like or what you do. Who remind you that you are worthy of being loved simply because you exist.

If you can't believe that, then you will never be wealthy.

T Stands for Time

What good is having a million or a billion dollars if your time isn't your own?

Time, to me, is freedom. You have structure in your day, in your quarter, in your year, in your next five years, in your next 10 years. How many people can't tell you where they'll be at 3 pm next Wednesday? I know exactly where I'll be at 3 pm next Wednesday because I treat my schedule with respect.

What would my life look like if I didn't treat my schedule with respect?

I'm a doctor in private practice, which means if I don't work, my staff doesn't work. How do you think it would go over if I said one day, "You know what? I think I'm going to the Bahamas for six weeks, and I'm going to leave tomorrow!"

But if in January of the same year, I decide that I want to spend November in the Bahamas, then I can plan ahead, and everyone knows. I can show the people who work for me and myself that I value my own time and that I respect theirs.

Emergencies happen, and part of true time freedom is building a life that allows you to do what you need to do when you need to do it. When Adrian was first diagnosed with cancer, I took three unscheduled weeks off, which no one begrudged me because, again, my toddler son had cancer. To me, time freedom is the luxury to exit when you need to. Even though I have a lot of expenses, I took those three weeks off when my son needed me. I took those three weeks off because my life is one where my time, unlike so many other things, is something I can control.

Here's another thing time freedom allows me to say:

Spending time with me is a luxury.

I have cultivated a patient population that is grateful to see me because I'm booked out for eight months. If you are a new patient and it is currently November 2021, then the earliest you will see me is in July 2022. It's a *luxury* that a patient can come to my office and see me.

The people who yell at my staff, who curse or leave me a one-star review because they asked for an appointment and were upset about the wait time or because they got a parking ticket when they were in my waiting room, these are the people who have shown me that they don't see my time as valuable, meaning they don't see *me* as valuable.

These are the same people who will scream at a flight attendant or lose their mind at a custodian but then fake niceness to the CEO of the same company. These are the people who have no respect for others and treat others unequally. You know what happens on an airplane if you lose your mind over a delay and you scream and threaten a flight attendant? You're put on a list, and you're never flying again. That is a prime example of a healthy boundary.

Because I have time freedom, I can say to this type of ungrateful person who shows up in my office, "Look, you don't have to see me. I'm not hurting for patients. I'm not hurting for business. You can see somebody else. It is not worth my time nor anyone else's here to see you. If you are rude to my front office staff on the phone, my nurses, my physician assistants or the management team, then you are rude to me, and I will not tolerate that kind of poor attitude and behavior."

Time freedom is about wanting to be exactly where you are and being exactly where you want to be. It's about looking at situations that don't serve you or bring you joy and then *leaving those situations.* It's about creating healthy boundaries in all areas of your life so that those who you allow into your world understand that it's a privilege. It's a privilege in the same way that flying through the air at 500 miles per hour to get to your destination in hours instead of driving for days is a privilege.

It's about loving yourself enough to know that your time matters and is limited on this earth because all those things are connected. It's about feeling confident enough to *act* like your time matters. You might have 100 years, or you might only have until tomorrow. Only God knows. So live in gratitude, service and joy, the way you were meant to live.

H Stands for Health

I don't know exactly what happens to our souls when we die. I do know that the soul is infinite—that long after you're gone from this earth, it enters whatever space that souls go, whether that's heaven, the universe itself, another plane of existence or something I haven't considered yet.

I do know for sure that everybody dies. Your body, at the end of the day, is a meat bag held up by a bunch of sticks. It's not going to last forever—it's not *designed* to last forever, which means you'd better take care of it while you can.

You may be an infinite soul, but your body is a temporary physical form.

It is challenging to explain the feeling of infinity that is your soul. Medicine, logic, the rational mind and Western science cannot explain it all. Your consciousness or soul or whatever you want to call it does not up and disappear when your physical form perishes. Your rational mind and ego will tell you it's BS when patients come back and talk about seeing the white light before they're shocked back into the world of the living. There's no scientific method or theory to explain something that we don't have the capacity to understand right now.

When patients are pseudo-dead, they're free from the body, which has physical pains. As a human being, you still have to eat, drink, pee and poop. Your bones hurt as you age —my patients tell me every day that I shouldn't get old. I jokingly reply that it beats the alternative, but now that I think about it, I will stop saying that. There's no under-standing the feeling of infinitely being a part of the universe unless you've experienced it yourself—by meditating your way there or through whatever your path was to that under-standing.

Death is something not to be feared. I know when I die, if I can choose to, I want to let go. I don't want anyone to guilt me into hanging out on Earth for another hour so they can see me intubated and sedated, unable to leave the bed to use the bathroom, let alone wipe my behind. Death, in my mind, is like taking off a tight surgical glove after a long case. It's the *ahhhhhh* of Bodhisattva in the heart sutra. It's the relief of the infinite soul escaping the limitations of the human physical form and going beyond.

Health is your first wealth, and you only miss it when it's gone—when you're too tired to play with your kid on a hot summer day or your shoulders scream out in pain because you spend most of your waking hours hunched over a computer.

Think about something small, like your taste buds: you can put fried chicken on them, or champagne, or a tomato fresh from your own garden. You taste those things and feel joy, but when was the last time you gave thanks for your taste buds for getting you there? If you burn those taste buds by taking a gulp of hot coffee, you won't be able to taste anything as intensely until they're healed.

I have another question for you: is there a limit to how much you can see in your mind?

I don't think there is. If you close your eyes and concentrate, you can see anything you want, whether it's a memory or a dream or something you only imagine in this very moment. You can place your awareness right up against the smallest, least perceptible sound in a room. You can put your awareness behind you, in front of you, to the left or to the right of you. You can bring your awareness inside of you to a point of pain in your body. To the feeling of the pressure of your feet touching the floor. To the heartbeat pulsing steadily in your chest. To the tingling of your fingertips.

Your body, though, is not infinite. Your body is a real physical form, and it carries real physical pains. The body decays until one day, you can no longer see things in your mind because the bag of meat holding it up doesn't work anymore. It's not a car where you can swap out the engine, where you have a seven-year warranty on the powertrain. When you blow a tire on your car, you can just swap it out for a new one. In a human body, when you amputate your leg, you can't just grow a new one.

I still have problems with my health, and I'm a doctor.

Again, I'm not here to judge you—but be honest with your-self. How many doctors are out of shape, smoking, drinking too much coffee or alcohol, using drugs as a coping mecha-nism and not getting enough sleep? How many doctors, instead of taking the Hippocratic Oath, take the hypocritical oath? They're doing the things they tell their patients not to do. And why? Because they don't own their time and don't know how to manage in any other way. But I promise you, there is no amount of fried chicken, alcohol or cigarettes to fill that void inside of you.

The external cannot fill the internal. Only the internal can. When you extend love, grace and compassion to yourself, then this dark hole begins to fill with light and take you back to a place of gratitude and joy.

When my wife was pregnant, I gained sympathy weight. If she had a middle-of-the-night craving for Taco Bell, who was I to refuse her? And if I was cruising through the drive-thru, shouldn't I just go ahead and grab a taco or two for myself so that we could enjoy our midnight snacks together? It felt good to fill the black hole of stress and lack of sleep inside of me with a chalupa wrapped in a quesadilla with an extra-large soda and miniature churros for dessert. The problem is that filling the hole in this way is temporary, and pleasure will give way to hunger again.

After Adrian was born, I was the heaviest I'd ever been. In January of 2020, I looked in the mirror and I didn't see myself. I saw a guy who wasn't taking care of himself, who wasn't expressing gratitude for his meat suit, who was taking it for granted instead.

I felt the very real limitations of my physical form. The discomfort of not fitting into jeans and other clothing that previously fit well. The icky feeling of a regular car seat belt hugging me tighter than before. The shame of having to undo a belt notch or the entire belt because I didn't maintain the self-discipline to stop eating when I was past the point of being full.

When I held up the mirror to myself, I started to make changes. I've lost weight, but that doesn't mean I'm done. Because what I learned from gaining and losing that weight is that taking care of your body is also taking care of your mindset.

If you're not taking care of your body—if you're drunk all the time, or you eat fast food for dinner every night, or the most exercise you get is walking from the car to the door of your office—you're not elevating yourself. You can't smoke and drink and eat fried chicken and expect to be feeling, looking and acting your best. Because there's a reason you smoke, eat fried chicken and drink. If you don't address those things, you will just continue to try to fill the void. But trying to fill that void with stuff from the outside world? It's impossible. You have to fill it from within using light from your fire.

I'm not here to body-shame you or tell you what to eat or not eat. I'm here to say there's a way for you to live your best life, whatever that looks like for you. Health isn't something only young people have, either. That's a fact we should all be excited about! Age should not be a limitation.

At Berkeley, I taught a chemistry lab as a sophomore—to freshmen! I created this elaborate backstory, saying I was doing research in a bio lab (which I was). I didn't tell them I was an undergraduate researcher because I didn't want them to take me less seriously.

As a doctor, I've had new patients come into the room and say, "Holy moly, doc—are you even old enough to graduate high school?"

Even my repeat patients tell me that when they refer their friends, they say, "You should see Dr. Tran and ignore the fact that he looks like he's 12, because he's really good."

There are also old geezers I roll with who would pose a serious challenge to me in a fight. The best fighter I knew when I was training in martial arts was 55 and kicking ass and moving faster than everyone (except me, of course). He was a Navy SEAL, and he was obviously committed to staying in shape long after he'd retired.

I was recently at my friend's pool party where the host, Darren McMahon, at age 55, did a crazy flip over our friend. Age really is just a number. You can treat your body like a temple wherever you are, whenever you're ready.

I bought a juicer recently, which I love, but I am not filling the void with juice. In fact, sometimes my mind craves fried chicken, and that's what I feed it. What I am trying to fill the void with, though, is WEALTH. When you're nurturing every part of your wealth, it grows. It grows and it burns, and someday I truly believe you'll climb so high you won't be able to feel the void at all anymore—you'll be so busy marveling at how amazing it is to be among the stars.

———

There's something else I want to say about wealth, illustrated by a story about my recent real estate purchase.

The house I bought had a shower stall in one of the bathrooms. The floor was patched, and I was told by a couple of handymen that it would be expensive to change—more trouble than it would be worth. They advised me to wait until one of the patches failed or there was an actual problem to be dealt with.

I decided that I would rather tear out the shower and make it beautiful because I could afford to but also because I noticed a few other patch jobs I wanted to clean up.

The shower stall came out—and guess what was behind it and the other patch jobs? Black mold growing due to the moisture.

Thank goodness I had decided to follow my gut and tear the shower out. The handymen are working, as I type, on installing a brand-new beautiful shower after tearing out the moldy insulation and applying bleach to everything. They also put concrete over the spaces where the mold had been growing, and I now feel a sense of relief about having my son, who is often in and out of the hospital and has a dangerously weakened immune system, breathe the air in our home.

There are always two ways to do something. You can do it the easy way and end up with black mold in your shower, or you can do it the right way (which is sometimes the hard way) and invest time, money and energy into building a bathroom with clean air. Wealth isn't something you can hack. If your health is failing or you're feeling lonely, you can't just slap a patch over those parts of your life and hope for the best.

Take the time to do it right. Take the time to do *everything* right.

That's when you'll truly be wealthy.

―――――

Emotions are like waves. They will rise, grow quite large and even crash against the shore, but then they subside and return to the vast ocean. To be on the shore can be a violent experience.

I remember as a child being knocked down by a wave in this unsafe space on the beach. It was a horrible cycle that started with a wave smacking me down, slapping my cheek against shells, rock and sand. Then, I was dragged toward the ocean with sandy, salty water filling every crevice of my body, only to be attacked again by another wave. Emotions can hit hard like this, feeling relentless and never-ending.

But you are not your emotions. You are not the wave. And you don't have to stand at the tide line, getting pummeled by wave after wave. You can place your awareness wherever you choose! You, as loving awareness, can select a safe location. You can be on the sand, chilling on a hammock between palm trees, watching the emotions come and go as waves do. You can stand safely behind the waterline, arms akimbo, chest puffed out as you watch the sunset.

Alternatively, you can pass the initial violence of the wave and swim through, beyond the shore. If you take your loving awareness and go further into the ocean, then you can see the waves as they come on.

Here, the waves won't crash you against the shore; instead, you can choose to jump with them or dive under them. You select a location of ease and flow—a beautiful state where you're having fun and weaving and bobbing with the waves for the sport of it. You're secure, and you maintain this feeling of comfort regardless of your external circumstances. The world may appear to rock around you, but you're just having a blast, enjoying the ride while avoiding danger.

You recognize that any emotion that comes your way is a wave— whether it's a surge of pleasure or a surge of pain. They all follow the same arc: they build initially, reach a peak and then subside.

This is why lottery winners will initially be happier than usual when they win but one year out, their happiness levels return to where they were before they won. It's why amputees are initially sadder than usual when they lose the limb, but one year later, they are at the same pre-amputation level of happiness.

The more that we feed into an emotion, the higher the wave can build. So anger, when fed, will grow larger and larger until it becomes a tsunami.

The more we resist the emotion, the longer it persists. So physical pain in your body, when you fight it and shout "Go away, pain!" only stays longer. As if the wave hits a peak and then plateaus. What you resist, persists.

This is because so much of pain comes from your own mind and ego. You create your own problems by resisting the way that things truly exist. When you love it all, just as it is right now, then there is no reason to have pain, worry, anxiety or discomfort.

So, if we can take a moment to breathe and let go of our illusions, our false sense of control and how we think things should be and instead love everyone and everything just as it is, then we can connect to our true nature—which is Love, Bliss, Light, Energy, God or whatever you want to call it.

SAFE!
HERE, YOU ARE
RIDING THE THOUGHT
AND EMOTION
WAVES WITH EASE
AND FLOW. PLACE
YOUR LOVING
AWARENESS BEYOND
THE
DANGER ZONE.

**NOT
SAFE!**
DANGER
ZONE!
UNAWARE –
OVERWHELMED
BY THOUGHTS
AND EMOTIONS.

SAFE!
HERE, YOU ARE THE
OBSERVER OR
WITNESS OF THE
THOUGHTS AND
EMOTIONS. PLACE
YOUR LOVING
AWARENESS BEHIND
THE DANGER ZONE.

Wealth isn't just money—it's everything you put out into the world and everything the world gives back to you. It is loving what you have, rather than hating what you don't. Wealth is peace of mind—it is carrying a feeling of safety and love in your heart that is available to you at any time, in any place.

EIGHT

We're All in This Together

Someone once told me that if your biggest problems are your personal problems, you need to get bigger problems.

Now, my personal problems at the moment are pretty big: I'm a doctor working during a global pandemic, and I have a huge real estate portfolio that I have to constantly stay on top of. I am a serial entrepreneur with multiple companies and employees. I am writing a trilogy of books, I run a coaching program, I am producing an album with my younger brother the musician, and I have a father who was diagnosed with a genetic heart problem that could affect me and my son as well. I have an uncle who was recently diagnosed with metastatic lung cancer, and as you already know, my two-year-old son is battling cancer.

But I also have so much. I have a loving family, a secure income, a job that lets me feel good about my contributions to society. I also have a hard-won outlook on life, one that pushes me to consider the role of my own ego in how I'm feeling. Once you've learned to put your ego down and live in an abundance mindset, a simple truth reveals itself: *we're all the same.*

I don't mean this in a corny "let us put aside our differences and see that on the inside we have so much in common with our fellow man" after-school special kind of way. I mean it literally: you, me, your family, my family, the trees that made the paper you're reading this book on. We're all connected, and that's why my problems are your problems and your problems are my problems. If people are starving, that's my problem. That's *everyone's* problem. Again, this might sound like lip service, but I really do believe we need to reframe our mindset to remember that there is a world outside our own egos and that we are part of that world.

That also helps me see that most of *my* problems are just problems of communication. If I'm having an argument with my wife, there's a 90 percent chance it's because of a miscommunication. If I miss a phone call with my team and have to reschedule but I'm also on my way into surgery, that's a problem of communication. Part of doing this work is opening yourself up to communication with the people in your life but also with yourself. Only then can I start to tackle the other 10 percent.

It's easy to watch the news at night and get overwhelmed. There is so much suffering and destruction in the world that tuning it out and saying, "That sucks but I have my own stuff to worry about" becomes the easiest option for most people.

And look, I am not saying that I want everyone reading this book to wake up tomorrow, sell all of their material possessions and dedicate their lives to bringing peace and clean water to the war-torn nations of the world (though of course if you *are* moved to do that, I'm proud of you!).

What I want you to see is that we're all connected. How much time do we spend trying to not connect with each other? Using screens, our cars, houses and our work as buffers? It's easy for my wife and I to watch Netflix together, and we both enjoy it. Netflix plays an important role in the wind-down portion of our evenings, but if that's the only thing we were doing together, we wouldn't be connected. Connections are living entities that need food, water and nourishment. You have to *try*.

We must recognize that beyond the boundaries of our immediate families, our best friends or our closest coworkers, we're still connected to everything and everyone else.

When is the last time you went outside for the express purpose of just being there? Just marveling at this natural wonderland we call a home planet and our role in it? In the early 20th century, an Idaho senator named Frank Church was trying to defend an area of back-country wilderness in his home state. He stood on the Senate floor and made these remarks:

> "The great purpose is to set aside a reasonable part of the vanishing wilderness to make certain that generations of Americans yet unborn will know what it is to experience life on undeveloped, unoccupied land in the same form and character as the Creator fashioned it. It is a great spiritual experience. I never knew a man who took a bed roll onto an Idaho mountainside and slept there under a star-studded summer sky who felt self-important that next morning. And unless we preserve some opportunity for future generations to have the same experience, we shall have dishonored our trust."

While I don't know what religion Frank Church practiced, I'm guessing it was different from mine, but that quote resonates with me because being in nature is a spiritual experience. Not only are you the same as other people, but you're the same as the trees and the water and the rocks and the stars.

It is the same DNA running through you that is read by the RNA polymerases that eventually are translated into proteins in the tree's cells, too. Our bodies are speaking the same language with the same alphabet; it's just being expressed differently. You have the same fundamental code that makes up your life. The trees create oxygen for you. They convert energy from the sun, and they have life as well. All these beings are living, and all these beings are one with each other, each playing its own small part in the magic of life on earth.

It's easy to feel the love of trees and to feel love for trees. They're beautiful, and they bring us shade, cool the air and sometimes bear delicious fruit we can snack on. My son Adrian loves trees. He runs up to them, gives them a hug and talks to them when we go for walks outside as a family. He shouts "Hello?" to the tree and then pauses and listens. It's very easy to feel love for the trees when witnessing this precious scene.

But what about loving someone you hate? Or something you hate? Because those things and those people are part of this world, too, and at some point, you're going to have to decide if you want to keep perpetuating that hate or if you want to release it so that it's no longer a burden you're forced to carry with you.

When I was in medical school, one of my classmates was murdered.

He was not a close friend, but I knew him, and he wore the same backpack I had. That made me think of us in some small way as brothers—him and I, the backpack twins. His name was Paul DeWolf, and he lived in a medical fraternity. There were around 20 medical students living there, and one day, three men in their 20s broke into the house armed with a gun and robbed the place. They took an Xbox, which was maybe worth $200 in cash, and somehow in the middle of the robbery, Paul woke up and struggled with them. Paul was shot, and he died.

For what? For $200? For an Xbox? The people who did this ended a beautiful life. Paul had an infectious laugh, a beautiful soul and planned on using his medical education to serve our country in the military. All of this was snuffed out. For nothing.

We all cried at Paul's funeral. During the time of the trial, I saw a picture in the newspaper of one of the defendants— probably younger than I was at the time—laughing. *Laughing.*

I was filled with rage toward this guy. "You ended my classmate's life for $200? What the hell is *wrong* with you?!" I thought.

What the hell *was* wrong with him? Meaning, what had gone wrong in this person's life? What brought him not just to Paul's fraternity house that night but to a place where he felt like robbing people with a gun wasn't just okay but was something he was entitled to do? Something he *had* to do?

I don't absolve this guy of what he did to Paul. He took something precious that wasn't his to take, and he'll never be able to give it back. But my hating him, my refusal to see him as a person with a life that led him to this dark moment, isn't going to bring Paul back, either. It's going to fester within me and make me less compassionate and less generous with my goodwill, all of which will hurt me.

I have to find, in my heart, love for Paul's killer. That's not easy. It goes against the ego. It goes against everything we've been taught about good and bad, right and wrong, reward and punishment. Why does Paul's killer deserve my love?

Because hate is a heavy thing to carry, and while releasing it is sometimes the hardest thing you'll ever have to do, once it's gone, you don't miss it. Hating him isn't going to bring Paul back. It crowds out the spaces where Paul should be. While we were not best friends, I knew Paul well enough to know that he wouldn't want that.

His family told me as I talked to them about this project that Paul's desire to become a doctor stemmed from a time when his older brother was hospitalized with a serious illness. Paul, just 10, found purpose in "playing doctor," and dreamed of growing up to help people like his brother get well.

Nothing will bring Paul back. Nothing will take away the hurt. You can decide in your soul to let go and forgive, and that's what takes it away.

Paul's family set up a memorial scholarship in his name. I've donated, and it means that every year someone will get to come to our amazing medical school and worry a little less about money—because of Paul. Paul's sister has two children, and that boy and that girl will grow up learning about Paul. Not just the way his life ended but all the things that made him who he was—what he loved, what foods he hated, what funny things he said.

When I think of Paul, I think of his face and his family, of the memorial I went to where his sister played the piano combining two pieces of music that were unrelated by genre: "River Flows in You" and the theme from *The Office* that somehow sounded beautiful together. I think of Paul's soul as a living thing that I can feel in this moment.

Every time I hear that Yiruma piano piece on Spotify or watch *The Office*, and I'm open and vulnerable with my ears and heart, the music brings me back to that moment at Paul's memorial. Like I said: Paul and I weren't best friends, but he made an impact on me. In talking about him now, I feel close to him. I feel like we are building a friendship that we didn't have time to build in life, and I know that none of this would be possible if I was still consumed with hate for Paul's killers.

I spoke to Thom DeWolf, Paul's father, as I was writing this book to ensure that I shared his story accurately and in a way that honors him and his memory. I am grateful for his feedback on this chapter and book, and I will let him speak for himself:

"Part of your theme in this section deals with anger and forgiveness. I struggled with this for months after Paul was murdered. It was intensified when the perpetrators were caught, and as you mentioned, their behavior in court. But that anger was internalized, and it was only damaging me. I knew that as a follower of God, I needed to forgive them for a number of reasons. I did not want to remain bitter all my life; I wanted to get better. I could not allow those murderers to continue to sap me of my happiness and joy in life.

In the class that my wife and I facilitate for those who have lost loved ones, I discovered there are different aspects of forgiveness. Once I realized that forgiveness does not condone an action, that consequences are still in place and responsible parties are still held accountable, I could begin to forgive.

At the trials, my wife and I soon realized that there was more than one life taken July 24, 2013. Sitting with the families of these individuals, we realized their sons would be taken from them as well. They were suffering a loss as well. We had compassion for them. The healing in our lives had begun, even before the sentencing. The fact that Paul is no longer with us is still a gut-wrenching reality. All the hopes and dreams we had will never be realized.

Paul's death pushed us even further into a "why is this happening to us" mentality. In the middle of those events, there was no good answer. There is still not an adequate answer for Paul having to lose his life in such a manner.

So again, we had to look for the positives instead of the negatives, or we would find ourselves again in the pit of bitterness that eats away at the soul. We had to let go of the hate in our heart, as you mentioned, and find a way to channel our energy. We found that in helping others who have suffered the loss of a loved one. Is this the path I thought we would be going down? Not at all. But what a blessing as we have been able to come alongside others who have suffered the loss of a dear loved one and been able to help them walk through their deep valley."

I have no words to convey the utter gratitude I have for Paul and his family for touching my life in the way that they have.

———

I have another mini-challenge for you.

Is there hate in your heart you can let go of? We don't

even have to start with hate—we can start with annoyance or low-level dislike. Is there someone in your life—a coworker, a relative, someone you interact with once a week—who takes up space in your head or heart and fills that space with negative energy?

What if you just…didn't? What if you took that hate and turned it into love that you radiated back out into the world? If you allowed yourself to think about that person's life and that person's choices and acknowledged that if you were them, you'd probably act the same way and say the same things?

I guarantee you'll get more out of love than hate, because hate will burn you out—it will corrode your insides like a leaky faucet does to your kitchen sink. Love is a flame that will keep you warm, energized and strong enough to move through the world as a person who understands how fundamentally connected we all are.

————

The more love you're willing to give, the more love you're going to get back. When you start to become a person who sees humans, animals, trees and stars as connected, you open yourself up to receiving their love in return.

The person I know with the brightest, clearest love energy is my son Adrian. We take him to Costco and sit him in the little seat for kids at the top of the shopping cart, and he just beams at people. And yes, I know, I have already talked a lot about Costco in this book, but I'm a 32-year-old dad who lives in a house in the suburbs. I spend a lot of time at Costco.

Strangers look at Adrian and are almost always moved to smile and wave because his delight at being out and about with his mom and dad is contagious. Sometimes people look twice and notice the fact that his hair is gone or that he has a feeding tube attached to his nose. Then they go about their days, thinking about the sweet little boy from Costco and hoping that whatever he's going through, he's strong enough to beat it. That's love energy, and it comes back to Adrian and our family.

My staff have all been very kind and supportive during Adrian's cancer diagnosis.

They are generous and give gifts even though they don't have the same means that I am fortunate to have. One gift, I believe, is the greatest one, and it's not material. My histotechnician is named Linda. Her father passed away last year, and it was very challenging for her. She experienced emotional trauma from the loss and held on tightly to the past when he was still alive. I guess you could say that she hadn't really dealt with the pain or processed all her feelings.

Then, one morning at work, she told me that she had a dream the night before. In her sleep, she saw her father at our clinic, her workplace. She knew that her father had passed away and wasn't sure if it was real, so she went to find a colleague to introduce him to. She found the dream version of me and brought me to her father, who gave me a warm smile, shook my hand, looked me in the eye and told me, "Your boy's going to be okay."

In that moment, she felt an overwhelming sense of peace and calm, and when she woke up, she had finally made peace with her father's passing.

Was it literally the spirit of her father in this dream? Some people might think so. Some people may say he came from the afterlife, or some might think he was reincarnated. Some people might think the whole thing is nonsense and chalk it up to her eating too much cheese before going to bed. I think these are all just ego and mental constructs, trying to take something that doesn't have one solid explanation and give it a structure our waking minds can understand.

What I do know for certain is that this appearance of Linda's father in her dream and in my life means that the universe is radiating love energy in my son's direction. He's connected to the universe, and the universe is connected to him.

Once we accept that we're all the same, that we're all bound together, and we lean into that, I think we also start to see these moments happen in real life.

Over Memorial Day weekend, Adrian had a fever with pancytopenia, meaning he had low red blood cells and platelets and his absolute neutrophil count, a measure of his immune system's ability to fight off infection, was trashed. In his state, a fever was an emergency that required hospital admission—an infection could be fatal since his body had no ability to fight it.

He had to be in the hospital to get antibiotics, fluids, close monitoring and cultures drawn to try and identify a source of infection. He also had to have several transfusions of packed red blood cells and platelets to try to bring those counts up. Since he is two years old now, they had a regular hospital bed for him to sleep in along with one of us parents. Typically, his mom sleeps by his side in the hospital, helping to comfort him when he gets scared or overtired. In past hospital stays, I had to be at work, but this time, I was there in the room with them.

On Sunday, early in the morning, my wife couldn't sleep. Adrian was restless. He was crying in his sleep, tossing and turning and kicking. He couldn't seem to get comfortable, which was the only way they both could drift off. Alicia was at the end of her rope and asked me to switch positions with her (I was sleeping on a pull-out chair next to them). So we did, and as soon as I lay in the bed with Adrian, he stopped stirring and slept peacefully. The week before, I had done an intense meditation, and I wondered if my calm energy was somehow making its way into Adrian, helping him relax in this stressful place.

I realized that I had to go charge my Tesla in case we got

discharged from the hospital, so I told Alicia that I was going to leave since Adrian had calmed down. I left to do so, and when I came back my wife was sound asleep in the hospital bed, so I returned to the pull-out chair.

Later, when she woke up, she told me that she was amazed and had never seen Adrian calm down with my presence before, as she was usually his main source of comfort. She also told me that when she went back to the hospital bed, she felt an immense sense of peace, calm and inner comfort. Instead of tossing and turning, as she had been the whole night, she fell asleep instantly. It was as if I had created a safe space and healing place just by lying in the bed there. As if my love for her and for Adrian had become so powerful that it was able to warm the bed for them, keeping them in the center of my heart.

This is what it means to turn your love outward. It might not come naturally at first, but when you commit yourself to it, you will literally see it change the lives of other people. First your closest family, and then your friends, and then, if you're open to it and lucky, you can change the whole world.

———

I recently bought a 77" OLED television. It's amazing—watching a movie at home is like watching a movie in a theatre, except the popcorn at home is 10 cents instead of $10. Even with sunlight coming through adjacent windows, the picture is still crisply displayed with no glare because each individual pixel lights up.

Now imagine that one pixel is the wrong color. Or simply went out. That's a personal problem. That's when you get caught up in your own head, your own story. You might think, "What the hell! I paid a few thousand bucks for this thing, and this is the quality I get!?"

But if you look at the whole screen, you would never notice. Because it's one tiny dot in a sea of eight million dots that are independently shining brightly to form the movie that is your amazing life, woven like a giant tapestry.

Another way to look at it if TVs are not your thing:

In medical school, we learn anatomy and physiology. We understand how the circulatory system works. I want you to ponder for a moment: what if a human being were just a red blood cell?

A red blood cell is born from the bone marrow and starts with a nucleus. This baby red blood cell sees everything as shiny and new and is as full of love and joy as a child. Over time though, the mature red blood cell loses its nucleus and its childlike sense of joy and wonder as it is released to do its job. The red blood cell has a singular function: to pick up oxygen in the lungs and deliver it to other organs in the body. It gets to see new and interesting things throughout the body from traversing the kidney to visiting the brain.

The red cell doesn't understand when its friends and loved ones pass away. When the platelet goes and sacrifices itself to heal an open wound in the body, the red cell asks, "Why is this happening? How is this fair?"

The red cell cannot see the big picture, that it was the platelet's purpose to die in order for the larger organism to survive and for all of the other blood cells and organs to continue living as well. The red cell itself only has a limited life span of maybe 100 days, and when it passes through the filter of the spleen and can no longer function in the capacity in which it was meant to, it is gobbled up and thanked for its service.

The red blood cell experiences the great privilege of living a meaningful life and playing a vital role to the larger organism, although to the red cell, it may feel like its job is not important when there are 25 trillion other red blood cells. The red cell can easily lose sight of its grand adventure when all it sees are the insides of the arteries, veins, capillaries, heart and organs. When it travels 66,000 miles seeing the body through its own experience.

The red blood cell never can get out of the body—it is trapped within the circulatory system unless the larger organism is injured or there is a problem. So, the red cell can never see the beauty of the eye or the human form when looking at the outside. It is only when the red cell expands its mind's eye that it can imagine the possibility of something bigger than itself. Or when the red cell is taken out of circulation and dies, then it is dissolved into the larger human organism again and can see things as they really are.

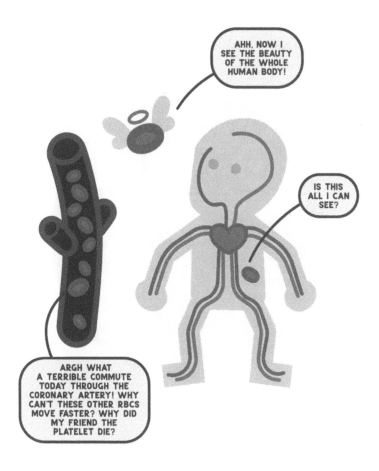

Finding love for other people: that's the universe. That's beauty and grace and love and joy. That's fire.

If this story moved you, scan the QR code below to donate to Paul DeWolf's memorial scholarship to honor Paul's memory. For my part, I'll be donating 10 percent of this book's first month of proceeds to the scholarship program as well.

NINE

Making Money Work for You

I have a question for you: what role does money play in your life?

There are no wrong answers here—in fact, I'd love for you to just shout out the first things that come to mind. (Afraid to shout and sound weird? Get over your ego. Nobody cares. You can be reading on the subway or in the quiet of your own home. Shout it out. Seriously!)

Does it stress you out because you don't have enough and feel like you need more? Are you intimidated by money—earning it, spending it and managing it? Are you the kind of person who logs into your online banking portal multiple times a day to make sure the numbers look the way they're supposed to? Or are you taking off to Vegas for the weekend, figuring you'll worry about bills next week?

Most of us, I think, fall somewhere in between those two extremes: we stay on top of things, but we don't necessarily have a ton of free time to devote to studying finance. We want to take care of our families, save for the future and treat ourselves to something nice every so often.

One of the tricky things about medicine and money is that jobs like doctor and nurse have long been held up as examples of "success," especially in America. Even if we set aside the TV caricature of the rich doctor living in a beachfront mansion and dating a series of supermodels, most people still think doctors have it made when it comes to cash. And many doctors do pull down high salaries.

Weatherby Healthcare, in its 2021 analysis of what doctors are earning, pegged the average plastic surgeon's salary at more than $500,000, with the average family medicine doctor earning just over $200,000. That is, by almost every metric, a lot of money! But for a lot of our colleagues, it also comes with high debt.

The average medical student's debt, according to think tank educationdata.org, is more than $200,000—and that's just for medical school, meaning if you've taken out loans to pay for an undergrad or master's degree, the number climbs even higher. This isn't even considering the opportunity cost of spending your prime early career days in school and graduating from the 25th grade. Recall that a dollar today is worth more than a dollar tomorrow due to inflation, so throw that into consideration as well.

The loan figures for nurses are a bit lower: according to Nerdwallet, the average student debt for a nurse with a master of science degree is around $50,000, with nurses who earn bachelor's and associate's degrees owing slightly less. That seems more reasonable, right? But per the Bureau of Labor Statistics, the average registered nurse earns around $75,000 a year.

These salaries are nothing to sniff at, but factor in things like loan repayment, cost of living, childcare and putting something aside for retirement and even $500,000 goes quicker than you might think. If you live in a big city on the coast with a high cost of living, support a large family and try to keep up with the Joneses by driving a nice car and sending your kids to private school, it's not hard to find yourself living paycheck to paycheck on a doctor's salary.

It doesn't help that we as a profession just don't talk enough about money. Seriously: one of the most important things I want you to take from this book is the idea that it's okay to ask (and answer) questions about finances—in fact, it's better than okay! Questions like:

- What is the economic reality of running your own practice versus taking an employed position?
- What's a fair salary for what amount of work? What's a good one, and what's a bad one? Am I being paid more or less than my peers for the same amount of work and productivity?
- Is it better to pay off loans first or start investing? Is it okay to invest while I still have debt?

I could go on because there's a ton of stuff about money so many of us are learning the hard way—that is, through messing up our own finances and scrambling to correct. No one will ever care about your financial health as much as you do, so in the same way I encouraged you to take ownership of your own thoughts in previous chapters, I want you to take ownership over your money and your financial future *now*.

———

What is the point of investing? There are two answers—one of them is philosophical, and the other involves a basic equation.

Let's start with philosophy.

Investing, or trying to grow the money you have into more money later, is about the future you want. It's paying off your loans early or putting your own kids through college. It's a once-in-a-lifetime trip around the world or helping a family member during a crisis. It's about—if this is what you want—

quitting your job and devoting your time to volunteer work or meditation or gardening.

That's why the concept of total WEALTH from chapter seven is so important. If you want to get rich for the sake of getting rich, you might get there. You might already have more money than me—I may be a millionaire, but I'm no billionaire. But if you don't have goals, what's the point? Part of learning how to lay down your ego and turn off the noise, I think, is to find those goals—to figure out who you really are and what values are going to drive the rest of your life.

Now, it's time to talk about the other part of investing, and to make it clear, I'm going to let Warren Buffett, one of the richest men in the world (and one of this country's savviest businessmen) tell you his number-one rule of investing:

"Don't lose money."

His number two rule?

"Don't forget rule number one."

Part of not losing money is not spending more than you earn and building up an emergency fund that will allow you to cover unforeseen expenses without going into debt. The other part of it is to beat inflation. This basically means that in 50 years you want your money to be worth more than it's worth today, and since you have no control over the federal government and its long-term fiscal policies, the best way to do that is to get your money multiplying *now*. That's going to require some work on your part, both in deciding how you want to put your money to work and deciding what kinds of investments you don't want to make.

This brings us to the stock market.

One way to *not* build wealth is by doing what a lot of people think is the best move: picking individual stocks yourself and thinking you'll be able to find The One that will make you rich.

How can you know whether a stock is going up or down at any given time? Are you familiar with security analysis or are you just making emotional purchases? You got a good feeling about a stock because you heard a hot tip from a random person like your uncle? Do you think you have more knowledge than the senators and other government officials who are briefed on confidential information such as the COVID-19 pandemic and are able to take advantage and dump their shares before the 2020 stock market crash?

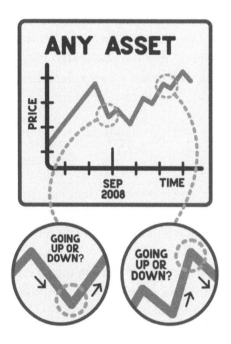

Unless you're Michael Burry and you can cripple hedge funds, don't mess around with securities that you don't understand.

Granted, Burry dropped out of neurology residency to become a full-time investor and open his own hedge fund. But if you're a full-time health-care professional, do you really think you're going to beat sophisticated hedge funds and people working 120 hours a week on the market research side?

You really think with even your fastest Comcast subscription, you will beat the hedge funds who have fiber optic wire placed so they can churn millions of transactions in between the time you click "sell" on Schwab and it executes in New York? Have you ever read an income statement or balance sheet? Do you really think you have more information than the guy who is subtly insider trading without alerting the SEC? And even if the playing field were level and everyone had the same information, do you even know how to use the existing information? Are you aware that there are armies of quantitative analysts (quants) who live, breathe and eat this:

$$\frac{\partial V}{\partial t} + \frac{1}{2}\sigma^2 S^2 \frac{\partial^2 V}{\partial S^2} = rV - rS\frac{\partial V}{\partial S}$$

And if you don't recognize that as the Black-Scholes partial differential equation and you're still thinking you're an expert stock picker, tell me what security you're buying: I'll be happy to take your shirt.

It helps to think of the market as a casino in this sense: it always wins! You might get lucky, but you probably won't. It's also way more stress than you need to take on, especially if you're just starting to earn a full salary after years of school and residency. The same goes for cryptocurrencies.

I've had some success there, but I only invested money I could afford to lose. It's not like I'm keeping Adrian's college fund in Dogecoin. You may be hyped up by social media, but where you put your money talks more than Twitter posts. Look at someone's actual financial holdings and status before you follow what they tweet. Elon Musk may be a fan of Doge, but there's a reason that Tesla bought Bitcoin and not the former.

So, if you're not picking your own stocks and hoping for the best, what are you doing in the market? I'll tell you what I would do if I were your standard FIRE guru: buy VTSAX and chill. That is, buy a basket of every single security traded in the New York Stock Exchange that is weighted by their market cap, so you own little slivers of Apple, Google, Netflix and so on. But even here, do you understand what index you're buying and why? Have you ever even read a fund's prospectus?

I would say that as a health-care worker, you should do the bare minimum, which is to save and invest in the stock market. You could dollar cost average into an index fund—that is, investing a set amount of money each month into something that will capture market gains over time while remembering that today's crash is tomorrow's soaring economy (and vice versa).

Buy when the market is low; buy when the market is high. Just keep buying until your portfolio's money starts making money. In short: play it safe. There's nothing wrong with playing it safe! If what you want is to work steadily and enjoy a nice retirement, conservative investing is probably going to get you there. It's a safe route to the moon—by horse and buggy.

When you start earning more, or your net worth grows to a certain point, you will receive the SEC designation of accredited investor. Then you will have access to high-risk, high-reward offerings that are not available to the general public because if you're not a millionaire, you can easily lose your shirt.

You might find yourself dealing with hedge funds or high-level money managers who work exclusively with clients who have a high net worth. The FIRE gurus and Bogle-heads will say that having a fund take one or two percent against your assets under management is a waste of money, but I would say it is worth it to pay a premium for those who can execute.

But what if you want to increase your net worth fast? What if you want to develop a passive stream of income, maximize tax advantages and set yourself up for FIRE? That's where alternative wealth-building strategies come in, and for me, the one that makes the most sense—and pays the highest dividends at the fastest speed—is real estate investing.

I get that as a concept, it's kind of scary: what if your tenants don't pay the rent? What if the roof collapses? What if you live in the San Francisco Bay Area and you had to save for five years for a down payment on your own primary residence? Well, off the top of my head, here are some answers to those questions:

What if my tenants call me about a leaky toilet at 2 am? What if they don't pay the rent?

First, let me say that I've never been bothered about a toilet in any of my properties. Second, if you're a doctor, then you have been, are actively or will be called about way more serious emergencies all the time about your patients. It would not be the end of the world even if you were self-managing and had to deal with a problem from a tenant directly.

Second, one of the most important parts of investing in real estate is building a team you can trust—a property manager who makes sure the lawn gets mowed and the basement doesn't flood (and if it does, that someone comes in and dries it out and mitigates the risk moving forward).

Someone who will handle all phone calls, so you never get called about a leaky or clogged toilet. Someone who can help you screen tenants to find the most solid candidates with good jobs and credit. But you also don't have to have individual tenants at all—you can invest in commercial real estate and rent space to large corporations, chain stores, even the government. Even a Home Depot can decide to stop paying you rent, but you're probably going to do okay with a publicly traded company as your tenant most of the time.

What if the roof collapses? What if there's a fire? Earthquake? Hurricane? Tornado?

You'll have insurance (or you should buy it). Also, since you'll be collecting rent every month, you'll have access to cash that you can use for repairs and maintenance.

What if you live in the San Francisco Bay Area and you had to save for five years for a down payment on your own primary residence?

There's no rule that says you must buy investment properties in the city or town you live in. Most of my income producing properties are out of state. I'm always paying attention to the real estate market in places outside of California to see what areas might make sense to invest in.

California is a pain because the taxes are high, the laws favor tenants and you can basically have squatters in your home forever. Imagine that you loaned your nice car to a friend, and he agreed to pay you $100 a day for it. Then he just kept the car and stopped paying you. And then he got drunk, hit someone with it, vomited in the back seat, totaled the car and ran away. That's what it can feel like if you have a bad tenant who trashes your property and stops paying you rent—and you can't evict them, or it takes forever to get them out.

Being a landlord gets demonized and it can create an apparent riff between the haves and the have-nots. Just put yourself in the shoes of the other party. There are landlords who do not care for their properties, and I've seen frankly dangerous living conditions like outlets that don't work, people running extension cords hundreds of feet for a light, non-licensed work and people trying to cram extended families of 20 into three-bedroom homes.

I've also seen tenants smash windows for being given an eviction notice after not paying rent for three months. It goes both ways. If you're a landlord, give your tenant a safe space to live. If you're a tenant, take care of the privilege of being in that home and pay the rent on time.

If you can set aside even a small portion of your salary each month, I think you'll find that a down payment, especially for a property in a market that isn't as hot as the ones in California or New York, is achievable for a lot of people working in the medical field. In Oakland, California, which gets a bad rap sometimes due to the housing shortage, a 1600-square-foot duplex can cost around a million bucks. That same duplex, if you transported it to Missouri, might be sold for $150K.

————

I was recently talking to a friend about the idea that humans sometimes act like we're wearing shock collars—like there's an invisible boundary we're afraid to cross.

Not long after, my wife told me about an experience she had. Meditating in the car (we have to find time where we can these days!), she had a vision of herself walking around in a yard, a patch of yellow grass. Beyond the yard was a long green field, and the grass extended to the horizon. As she moved towards the farthest reaches of the space, she felt a shock—an electrical shock.

Later that day, she went to the pharmacy to pick up medicine for Adrian. The drug he needed was out of stock, and she was worried she wouldn't be able to get it in time. It was stressful at first, but she suddenly felt confident and calm, sure she'd be able to solve the problem (which, by the end of the day, she did).

She told me that during this experience, she realized what her vision while meditating earlier in the day meant. The shock she felt at the border was her own fear, and that there was no reason that she could not step over into the field of grass. That she and humankind are all limitless, and that when she put her mind to something important, it would get done no matter what.

Discomfort is the development of your dreams—that's why they're called growing pains. There is a future version of you that has already breezed past this obstacle, so connect with that higher Self. Choose to show up as the version of you who decides to push past the point of resistance and go beyond your fears and self-imposed limits.

TEN

Playing to Win

When I was growing up, I loved watching *The Simpsons*. It's been on forever and I hope it stays on forever, and that sometime in the not-so-distant future, I'm watching it with Adrian on Sunday nights.

There's a scene that to this day is lodged into my brain. The Simpson family gathers around the table for board game night. They settle on playing Monopoly, and before you know it, the game has descended into chaos. Homer is strangling Bart, with Marge and Lisa trying to pull them off each other, while Maggie, the baby, pushes a special panic button designed for exactly this purpose. When the cops show up, they have a conversation they've clearly had 100 times before.

"Oh, another case of Monopoly-related violence," one cop says wearily.

"How do those Parker Brothers sleep at night?" his partner asks.

I love Monopoly, and I love that it isn't just a board game. If you pay attention, it becomes an easy way to understand exactly how to invest in real estate. I want to walk you through some lessons I've learned on the Monopoly board, which will allow you to visualize yourself doing your own wheeling and dealing.

Are you ready? Collect your $200 and let's go!

Start Small, Think Big

When you want to win in Monopoly, one of the first things you must learn is that you have to start buying up the lower-status (and lower-value) properties. I think a novice—in Monopoly or in real-life real estate investing—would run into the problem that these investments don't always scream instant wealth.

In Monopoly, the cheap properties cost $60 to own, and they only deliver $2 in rent. It doesn't seem like it's worth it, but I promise you, it is—you can't have a monopoly (or a successful real estate portfolio) without starting and getting on the board. Once you buy one of these properties, it becomes easy to buy others; before you know it, you own everything on the block.

Whether your growth is linear or exponential, your first point is still coordinate (1,1)—and from there, you can decide to scale at whatever pace is right for you.

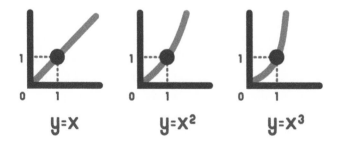

Two dollars quickly becomes $4. Because in the game, your rent doubles when you own a monopoly. But the real benefit in owning a monopoly is you can start to develop the land. You can put houses and hotels there, and sooner rather than later, you're collecting $20 every time someone lands on one of your squares.

So, how does this translate to real life? The lesson here is that you want to invest early and often. You've got to start somewhere. Unless you inherited a ton of property, you're not going to own a giant complex or shopping center right out of the gate. You don't yet have the capital to go out and buy a casino or a chain of hotels (though if you do, call me!).

Your first deal should be relatively small, which is good! You need to start learning how to buy assets. Assets, at their simplest definition, are things that put money in your pocket every month. My personal belief is that for a physician, your first income property or investment property in real estate should be a small residential multi-family unit, specifically a duplex.

You don't want to buy a single-family home, because then —especially in markets like the one we've been dealing with in 2020 and 2021—you'll find yourself competing with people who are looking for their dream homes. A dream home is an emotional buy, which means people are willing to spend more money to get a property under contract. For you, it's a number; for them, it's The One. When you're looking at any investment, whether it's stocks, bonds, real estate or cryptocurrency, it will benefit you to think logically. You're not here to live in these properties; you're here to make money, and remembering that will make deals a lot easier to parse.

Cash In, Cash Out

In Monopoly, what are the best squares to own? I think everyone knows the answer: Park Place and Boardwalk. If you're lucky enough to land on the latter of these spots, you get the opportunity to spend $400 to buy it from the bank. Once you cough up the money, it's yours. There's no mortgage on it. You don't have to make monthly payments. And now, anytime someone rolls the dice and lands on Boardwalk, they owe you $50 in rent.

These numbers allow us to calculate and evaluate investments against each other. Whenever you look at investments, you want to compare apples to apples. It's hard to say, "What is the income produced by this duplex compared to this triplex or a self-storage facility? Or a medical office building versus a single-family home or 100-unit apartment complex?" It's challenging to compare apples to oranges. But if you get down to the raw numbers, then you can compare apples to apples. One way to do that is called cash-on-cash calculation.

That means you're looking at how much money you get back for the cash that you put into a deal. For Boardwalk, you spend $400 once and own that asset forever. Any time your rivals land on Boardwalk, they owe you rent. So, the first time somebody lands on your Boardwalk property, you get $50. From there, it's easy fractions: 50 over 400 reduces to one over eight, or 12.5 percent. That means your cash-on-cash calculation is 12.5 percent.

In real life, this translates to you growing your portfolio by 12.5 percent year over year, which is a healthy return.

Let's say you own a real-life duplex, and we'll do the calculation again, adding a few zeroes to everything. You buy a duplex in Texas, and it costs you $400,000, which you have in cash because you've been living on a portion of your salary and saving the rest. Then you plug in the same numbers: if your duplex is producing $50,000 per year net and you spent

$400,000 upfront to buy it, then your cash and cash return is 12.5 percent.

A lot of people—even doctors and nurses who have done years of post–high school science work—are afraid of math. But this isn't advanced calculus we're doing here! When it comes to budgeting for life and evaluating real estate investments, the math is not difficult. These are skills you learned in elementary school. We're just using different names and operating with bigger numbers. You can get fancy and think about more complex variables, but it's nothing that is outside the skill set of a physician (or most people who graduated high school). I'm also writing this in 2021, which means there are apps and calculators and spreadsheets that will do the math for you. You don't have to do math to get into real estate if you don't want to! You just have to insert the correct number in the correct place.

Let's look at another example. Say you didn't land on Boardwalk, but instead on its ever-so-slightly less sexy neighbor Park Place. Park Place costs $350, and the rent that it generates when somebody else lands on it is $35.

So again, let's put the rent on the top of the investment. $35 divided by $350 is 35/350 or 3.5/35, or 1/10 or 0.1, which is 10 percent cash on cash.

What if you've landed on both properties and were lucky enough each time to have the cash on hand to buy them? In Monopoly, when you own all properties of the same color, the rent on each of them doubles.

If I own Boardwalk and Park Place, when somebody lands on Boardwalk again, instead of paying $50, they owe me $100. And if we're going to calculate the cash-on-cash return for somebody landing on Boardwalk, then the rent paid to you is $100.

To purchase both, you had to pay $400 for Boardwalk and $350 for Park Place. Add those together and you get $750. So that's 100/750, or 10/75, which is 13 percent cash on cash.

That's a better return than you'll get in the stock market if you held a low-cost index fund for a long time, making this collection of assets a smart one to hold.

From there, you can start developing. It costs $200 to put a house on Boardwalk, which is a pretty penny—but if you have it? Everyone who lands on Boardwalk has to pay you $200. That's a *100 percent cash-on-cash return* at 200/200.

"But Patrick," you're saying, "I had to spend money to buy the actual property!"

Which is fair, especially if we're applying these lessons to your real life. The rent you're collecting is $200, which you'll put atop your total investment of $950, which equals 21 percent cash-on-cash return. It's not 100 percent, but it's still spectacular. You'd be very happy to pay a hedge fund a two percent management fee to get you a 21 percent return on your money.

With the existing equity in the properties, there is also an opportunity to sell in cases of significant market appreciation. Say I bought a duplex for $120,000 last year. I put 25% down of the purchase price to represent 25% equity in the property ($30,000). The bank financed the rest of the purchase, meaning the bank's loan to me is 75% of $120,000 or $90,000 total with associated interest and amortization over 30 years.

Now, the property doubles in value to $240,000, which is realistic with a value add play or if you let five years go by with local appreciation. If I sell the property for $240,000, then I get the home's $90,000 loan paid off—or whatever was left of it after servicing that debt over the time period. After that, I keep the remaining $150,000 minuses taxes, closing costs and other expenses of course. At a high level, I collect almost $150,000 for doing minimal work: $30,000 from the down payment, $120,000 in equity.

There are also selling expenses from the closing costs, and the rehab budget. Realistically, you could expect $15,000 in selling costs and $15,000 in rehab that you put into it. Oh, and don't forget taxes you pay, which are probably either 15% or 20% if you're a physician. Assuming the highest bracket, then you get $72,000 back to you. Still, not a bad profit!

Assets that increase in value also increase your equity in them. Let's say that in my imaginary $120,000 duplex, I have 25% equity and the bank has funded 75%. Now, the bank loan doesn't increase—it's still $90,000, so I now have 62.5% equity! Now, say I want some of that cash in my wallet or to use to buy another $120,000 duplex. Now I tell the bank, "Hey, I want to cash out refinance." This means they will give me a new loan of 75% of the $240,000, which equals $180,000 loaned and $60,000 back to me. Thus, I get all of the cash back from before ($30,000) plus a cool extra $30,000 in my bank account. Now, my profit is freed from the money jail of sitting in the duplex without having to sell the asset and trigger a capital gains event. This is tax free cash! Recall that if you sold at long term capital gains, you would have had a drag of 20%. The cash out refinance can be a powerful strategy to making your money work even harder for you!

You Have to Play to Win

The second lesson of Monopoly is that if you don't invest your money, you will never win. You'll be paying rent and saying goodbye to your dollars without any coming in to offset those costs. There's no way in hell you're going to make enough money running around the board, trying to collect $200 to pass Go every time. There's the Community Chest option, but the money you can get from that isn't likely to be big. You might get $10 for winning a beauty contest or $50 for acting as the Chairman of the Board.

If you have a W2, you are trading time for money. You must clock in to work at 8 am, clock out at 5 pm and make the salary you agreed upon when you took the job. If you're not doing that, then you don't get paid. There's no money coming in. Just as you work, so too does your money. Money doesn't just magically multiply; it has to clock in, too. If you're holding all of your money in a savings account that isn't keeping up with inflation or hiding the money in your mattress or a safe, you will never become rich. You will never build wealth. In fact, you are *losing* money every second those dollars are not put to work.

The government prints more money, which causes inflation. The cost of goods rises. As a result, everything starts to cost more money over time. If you happen to find yourself a time machine, you'll very quickly learn that a dollar today is worth more than a dollar tomorrow. And a dollar 20 years ago went a lot further than a dollar today.

That's all due to inflation. It's a trap that even smart people sometimes fall into. They get excited that real estate appreciates, for example. They might say, "Okay, I bought my house for $300,000 30 years ago and now it's worth $2 million." That can seem very exciting, but with inflation, you learn that the spending power of $300,000 in 1970s dollars is equivalent to the spending power of $2,100,000 in 2021 dollars. So again, we have to compare apples to apples. If you bought your house in the 1970s, you probably paid a lot less money than what the house would sell for in the market today in terms of the absolute value of the list price.

It's not enough to just save your money. You have to *grow* your money. You have to make your money work for you; otherwise you'll be working for it—forever. That sounds dramatic, but it's true. And I don't know about you, but I don't want to work until I die. I want to live a life that is full of meaning, joy and service. I also don't want to fall into the habit of thinking that more money means more happiness. This is worth saying again, even though I've said it more than once already: *money will not bring you happiness.*

Which is why—and I get that this sounds strange—you have to make your money do the work. When your money is working, you're free to spend your time building and living the life you want.

Hitting and Missing

In the 19th century, a lot of people got rich buying oil companies or starting railroads. You, however, don't have to bother with those things.

In 2009, a business student won the Monopoly world championship in Las Vegas, where the grand prize was $20,000. For playing Monopoly!

His advice: you shouldn't buy the utilities or the railroads because you only have a 3 percent chance of making money from them.

Here's my real-world parallel: commercial real estate investing can be very hit or miss. In real life, if you buy a big commercial office building, you have a big mortgage. If nobody lands on the railroad or the utility, or nobody lands on your real-life commercial office building, you're stuck with an asset that isn't earning any money. Very quickly, that asset becomes a liability, where it takes money *out* of your pocket every month. As I write this in mid-2021, many American cities are just now starting to see office workers return after the great work-from-home reshuffling caused by the COVID-19 pandemic. What do you think your bank account balance would look like if you owned a 20-story commercial office building in the heart of New York City after 18 months of expiring leases your tenants chose not to renew?

You must be very careful and critical in evaluating an asset class that has a long turnover time. For me, it's like this: anyone can buy a home. Anyone can buy a small, multi-family property like a duplex or a quadplex. Eventually, one can buy a shopping center in a busy community that will always have banks, pharmacies and grocery stores. Everyone in real life *can't* buy a utility company like an electric company, a water company or a railroad.

Large-scale commercial properties are a different game, and they behave differently. You can very easily lose your shirt, or at the very least, spend a lot of time worrying, which is exactly what I want to help you avoid.

Getting Out of Jail

In Monopoly, it's okay to go to jail late in the game. Think about what the board looks like when the game is almost done. Every property is bought up, and people have built houses and hotels. Every roll, there's the possibility that you're going to be the one ponying up $2,000 for the privilege of stopping on Atlantic Avenue decked out with a hotel.

Depending on how you've been playing, this might mean you're going to go bankrupt. Wouldn't it be nice to take a little break right about now? The rules of the game state that you can go to jail by rolling doubles three times in a row or pulling the famous card: Go to Jail, Do Not Pass Go, Do *Not* Collect $200. On paper, it doesn't sound ideal. But in the game, when everyone owns everything, your trips around the board are like walking on eggshells, and you're just hoping that you don't land on a property so developed that you lose all your cash.

I should be very clear: this isn't going to be a literal lesson in which I advise you to go to jail.

What I want is for you to recognize that there are different stages in your life and different stages of the Monopoly game. Early in the game, going to jail sucks. You don't get the chance to evaluate the real estate deals as you roll the dice and walk around the board. You're not in the game. It's those early rolls —and those small properties—where you're laying the groundwork for your eventual empire.

Investing in real estate, if that's the path you want to pursue, is something you should be doing early and often. It's like they always say: the best time to plant a tree was 20 years ago. The second-best time to plant a tree is right now.

What is it going to take for you to buy your first income property? What is it going to take for you to decide to change your life? You don't want to wait any longer than you've been waiting.

When it comes to going to Monopoly jail late in the game, if you've played smart, you have nothing to worry about. Your wallet is full of that pink and blue money, and since you can't go anywhere, you don't have to part with it.

Life, as we all know, includes very few moments that don't cost money, time or energy. Let's say you have a nice home, but the roof collapses and it's not covered by your insurance. In an instant, you have to spend $20,000. The same way that your beautiful new McLaren $300,000 car could be the victim of a hit and run by a tourist bus in a parking lot when you're not around, and now you're stuck picking up the pieces and paying for repairs out of your own pocket.

Here's another hypothetical: you're a doctor and you think you have job security, but there's a global pandemic. Your hospital employer fires you because of this act of God, and they're just trying to survive the crisis. Your family depends on your income, and you have none.

The liquidity, or the cash you have on hand, can quickly become tested. If you don't maintain an emergency fund, if you don't have a little bit set aside, then what are you going to do when the shit hits the fan?

If you want to invest in real estate, I want to help you. I want you to make money and have fun! But I also want you to consider having an emergency fund that you have easy and quick access to. Again, all of this is pointless if you're just going to end up more stressed and more burned out.

Think of your emergency fund as a box of matches you can use to relight your fire when you feel it flickering and dying.

Friends or Foes?

Monopoly, as we know from *The Simpsons*, is a fundamentally competitive game. For every property you buy, there's one you lose—and when it comes to owning the game's most desirable lots, it's every person for themselves.

The people you're playing against want to make more money than you. They want you to go bankrupt. They want to develop land. And they want you to sit in jail with nothing. The way you protect yourself in the game is twofold: first, you're buying properties and building houses and scoring monopolies of your own. Second, you're going on the offensive. If one of your friends or family members needs to secure Baltic Avenue to hold a monopoly and you land on it? Guess who's the new landlord for that section of the board?

In real life, you want to protect yourself from downside potential. While it's sort of fun to imagine another literal translation here, I'm not advising you to buy up everything anyone else wants to buy whenever you get the chance. That would be bad financial advice, and it would be bad advice for being a good and respectful member of society.

Here's an example you can use: right now, the cost of building a new home is higher than it's been in decades. Lumber, among other commodities, is incredibly expensive—a $20 piece of plywood a year ago now costs way more, with prices climbing 300 percent or more during the pandemic.

You're investing in properties that already exist as opposed to buying new ones, but this still matters for you. If your duplex needs repairs, there's a good chance you'll need to buy some lumber! If you want to build a new home, it will cost more than any existing home on the market. The cost to build a new home in 2021 is much higher than it was in 2020 due to multiple market forces outside of your personal control.

My super savvy real estate and hotel developer friend Jake Harris, author of the best-selling book *Catching Knives: A Guide* to *Investing in Distressed Commercial Real Estate*, found that it was cheaper and faster to source lumber from brokers in Europe (specifically Nordic Spruce for heavy timber beams and columns) and sail it across the Atlantic Ocean to build a mixed-use project in East Austin than to rely on his previous vendors and local suppliers. This saved the project and its investors millions of dollars during a global pandemic in which many people were losing their shirts.

Here's one way that you could capitalize on a lumber bubble: buy cheap houses that are less expensive to own than to build new. That is, pick up a tiny single-family home in Indiana for $20,000 when the price of lumber to build that same home is substantially higher. Or, put some more zeroes behind that number, depending on your liquidity or appetite to raise capital, and buy a casino on the Las Vegas Strip that would cost more to rebuild than what you bought it for, thanks to COVID-19 keeping everyone at home and tourists away.

Now, I'm not telling everyone to go out and syndicate apartment buildings and casinos, but what I am saying is that opportunities abound in this world if you keep an open mind and an open heart. It's not like you screw over the guy who is selling at a desperate time. It can be a win-win situation, which I believe is the best way to do business.

Imagine you're a hotel owner and about to go bankrupt. You can't afford to pay the mortgage, and the bank is going to start garnishing your wages if you can't pay the bills. Maybe you're a doctor and real estate investor, but you made a bad call with this hotel and now have debt service of $10,000,000 to the bank. You already paid $4,000,000 and have that much equity and bought the building at $14,000,000. Then it's 2008 or there's some sort of market force that cripples the economy, and the building you bought is now worth only $12,000,000. Or $10,000,000. Or $8,000,000. Yet, you still owe money on the $10,000,000 note to the bank. Your debt service is around $700,000 a year, and time is running out before that note is

due. You're about to lose big, and are probably feeling significant pressure.

Then I come along and say:

> Hey dude, I'm sorry you're in this bad situation. I love your
> hotel, but it's unfortunately not worth the $14,000,000 you
> paid for it right now. If you had the liquidity to withstand
> the market coming back over a period of years, then you
> wouldn't sell. You'd pinch pennies and survive the storm,
> and one day, your building would be a good investment.
>
> In 20 years, it would be paid off, worth $20,000,000 and
> you would own it outright with no debt to the bank. It
> would be a great deal in that situation. But you're not in
> that situation—you're about to file for bankruptcy. Let me
> throw you a rope, because you picked a bad time to buy the
> place and you're about to drown. I'll swoop in and hand
> you a check for $10,000,000 in cash because I can afford it
> and you can't. And now, the bank will stop harassing you.
> Yes, you lost $4,000,000, but at least you didn't lose
> everything. You gained a life lesson that you were over-
> leveraged, and maybe you'll be more careful in terms of
> keeping capital reserves for a rainy day.

When it comes to residential housing, a lot of states are
seeing record low inventory. Everyone wants to buy a home,
and everyone feels like they can't—a recent *New York Times*
article interviewed one couple who made offers on nearly 100
homes and decided, after losing out on all of them, to keep
renting for a while. People are writing these insane offers: cash
only, waiving all contingencies from inspection to appraisal to
financing.

Don't do this! Don't do it with residential property, and
especially don't do it with commercial property. Learn to trust
but verify. This is called due diligence, and it means doing
your homework and understanding the full picture of what

you're buying before you sign the contract. You wouldn't buy
a new car without making sure it has the engine it needs to
drive off the lot. The same goes for real estate: you do not
want to spend everything you've got on a shopping center only
to discover after you've closed that it's infested with termites or
that no tenant has stayed for more than a year.

Part of playing both offense and defense means staying
aware of what's going on, which a surprising number of
people don't do. Pay attention to market trends locally, regionally, nationally and globally. The world is becoming increas-
ingly connected. A butterfly flapping its wings in Florida may
cause a tsunami in Japan, and Japanese banks needing to
demonstrate profits to their investors can sell off United States
Treasury securities (government bonds) and drive down face-
value prices of bonds while increasing yields.

If you invest out of state, make sure you're not having the
wool pulled over your eyes because you're an unsophisticated
out-of-state buyer from the Bay Area, where you're used to a
duplex in Oakland costing $1,000,000. If you are, it probably
makes buying a triplex in Nebraska for $100,000 look like the
steal of a lifetime. The $100,000 may be a good or bad deal,
but you can't compare it to the duplex in Oakland. Again, you
have to compare apples to apples. If you're out of state, you
need to build a local team you can trust to walk the property
and make good decisions on your behalf.

You don't have to fly out and walk into a property to see if
it's a good deal or not—there's FaceTime, recorded video,
inspections teams, banks that are FDIC insured, cities and
county deed recordings that are all a part of a real estate
transaction. So you can definitely rest easy that you're buying
a property that exists and that it's not some huge conspiracy
for you to buy a vacant property. But many people in this
process are not committed—they are merely involved.

Ajahn Brahm tells a story of marriage being like the
difference between the chicken and the egg and the pig and

the bacon. The chicken is involved. The pig is committed. The same goes for real estate: when you have skin in the game and money in the deal, *you* are *committed.* Anyone who is making money off you or is a part of your team is *involved.* The only person who will be the best steward for your money and look out for your best interests financially is you. You have to take ownership of your life, your money and your investment deals. Above all, use your head. If something seems too good to be true, it probably is. But fortunately, you'll do all the due diligence and avoid daydreaming about how magical owning *this* particular property is going to be for you.

Seriously: you've got this.

Risks and Tradeoffs

In Monopoly, you don't want to give away your strategy. The same applies to your real-life, real-world, real estate invest-ment journey. You do, however, want to be honest: with your partners, with your tenants and with yourself. The sooner you can shed your cognitive biases and your attachments to your ideas about why you won the game before or why you were successful at investing before, the sooner you can make the space to make honest assessments of your opportunities. From there, you'll build wealth faster and continue to improve.

Let's say you played Monopoly for the first time with no strategy, and the two things that stick out in your mind about the game are that you won and that you bought the Electric Company.

Let's say it happens again. You bought the Electric Company and won. Maybe it even happens a third time. But recall that correlation is not the same as causation. And now, before your next regular Monopoly game, you're here, reading this book. The next time you play, are you going to buy the Electric Company even though we've talked about why it's a bad idea and I've shown you other squares that will be way more profitable in the long run?

It would be a logical fallacy for you to go and buy the Electric Company now that I've explained to you that it's not the best way to win Monopoly. But life is not always about winning. Playing a board game is not always about winning. If you want to just have fun and buying the Electric Company brings you joy, who am I to tell you not to do it?

What I am telling you is that if you want to win, the way to do it is to play logically. Investing in real life is the same way. When it comes to buying a primary residence, there are a lot of factors that don't come down to fractions. It's about peace of mind. It's about your personal preferences and comfort and desires that you have for yourself and your family. Your dream house isn't your dream house because it's a Hollywood media mogul's dream house—it's because it's *your* dream house.

I love my spa, and I'm so happy we found a house that came with one. But if you have twin toddlers who get into everything and are always running just out of your sightline, my dream spa might be your worst nightmare. Everything is a risk and trade-off in life. You just need to know what game it is that you're playing.

When it comes to investing in real estate, the game you're playing is one in which the winners are at the intersection of maximum profit and minimum headache. Once you identify potential investments that sit at that point on the axis, you can ask the questions that transcend numbers on a spreadsheet.

Is it going to help me accomplish my goals and realize my full potential? Is it going to take me closer to my vision of how I want my life to look, how I want my net worth to grow? How does this fit into my long-term plans not just for my portfolio but also for my family, my business and my personal goals?

Those aren't questions that usually come up during Monopoly. But once you win that game, you can shift your focus—to the game of life.

If you want to build an empire, you always start with your first one. You must get on the board before you can play the game. Decide first, then act. Learn the rules of how to create abundant wealth and joy in your life.

The rules are the rules for a reason. Sometimes they bend, and sometimes they break. But a solid foundation in how to play the game will pay dividends for the rest of your life.

ELEVEN

The Work Continues

Lately, I've been waking up early—like 4 or 5 am early. Why? As busy as I am, shouldn't I be taking every possible opportunity to rest?

For me, those morning hours are better than rest because they're *mine*. Adrian and my wife are sleeping, my patients are sleeping and my email is quiet. It's my time to meditate, to contemplate, to think about what I want to get out of each day. It's my time to do things like write this book, nurturing the part of myself that wants to wrestle with big ideas and try to put some of my feelings, hopes and dreams onto the page.

It's also my time to go outside. If I take a walk, I might see a shooting star or something else so beautiful it takes my breath away. I feel like when I go outside, I am floored by nature, whether it's a bird or some new flower in a yard I've walked by a thousand times.

Then, I get ready for work. I spend what morning time I can with my wife and son and then it's off to spend a full day seeing patients and performing surgery. When I come home, Adrian and my wife are always excited to see me, and it's important that I spend at least 20 or 30 minutes just decompressing—shaking off the noise of the outside world and turning my focus inward to my happy family and my happy home.

As the night winds down, we get Adrian ready for bed. We have a whole routine: he loves our fish, and he likes to help us feed them before bed. He puts his little fingers in the fish food and sprinkles it into the aquarium.

We try to brush his teeth. He's been resistant recently because I think he's nauseous from his chemotherapy, but we try as best we can, and then we read him a book. He gets his soft little weighted Mickey Mouse that one of my friends got him when he was in the hospital. He'll cuddle with that and a soft blanket, and then we turn on the night-light and the music. Then we give him a kiss, and it's bedtime for him.

After he dozes off, I might do a little work or make some calls, and then my wife and I spend time together. It would be so easy for us not to do this—to only be together when we're with Adrian or when we're doing errands and chores. But our connection is vital to both of us and to our family unit, and it's worth it to make the effort—to go to bed at the same time, together.

I tell you all of this not because I think the minutiae of my day is that riveting but because I want to explain, using myself as an example, a Buddhist saying that resonates strongly with me:

Before enlightenment: chop wood, carry water. After enlightenment: chop wood, carry water.

That first time I seriously meditated, when I felt myself ask questions of the universe and felt the universe answer back, my whole life changed. It was like every fiber of my being had been rearranged somehow, and I can say with certainty that today, I am a very different man than the one I was a few years ago.

But do you know what I did after that transcendent experience? I went home. I helped my son get ready for bed. I woke up and went to work. I chopped wood and carried water.

Enlightenment, inner peace or true happiness? Those aren't fixed destinations. It's not like you wake up one morning and think, "I've figured out the secret to true wealth! Time to spend the rest of my life doing something else." You have the privilege to work at it, consistently. I *get* to work at it, consistently.

I'm constantly being pulled in different directions. Sometimes this is due to external factors, but sometimes it's just because I have a million ideas, and I want to execute them all *now*. For me, then, holding on to the beauty I've been able to access goes hand in hand with living in the moment.

I know that at the end of the day, when you look back from your deathbed, you're not going to think, "I wish I'd spent more time on business calls." I do these calls with my team because I'm trying to build a kingdom for long-term wealth and security for my family. You have to remember *why* you're doing whatever it is you do. It's easy to get excited about a big real estate deal, and it's easy to get lost in it—to feel like the thrill of the score is what you're after. That's not what I'm after, though, and I must work to remember that every day.

I didn't always get it. I let myself get so busy that my wife had to say, "Hey, you're not being present. You're so busy building this thing that you're not spending quality time with Adrian like you were before."

I listened to her and thought: "You know what? You're right."

So, I leaned into blocking off time on my calendar for work and time for family, and I guard that boundary with my life. Because when I'm with Adrian, crawling around on the stairs, or lying on the carpet while he runs his Hot Wheels cars on me like I'm a road? It's such a gift to get that time with my sweet little boy, to make him laugh and show him that his father loves him more than anything else in this world. It is a *gift*, and it's one I never want to take for granted.

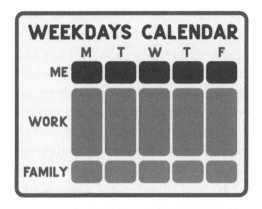

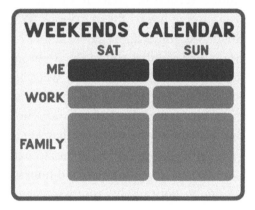

And you know what I can't wait for? When Adrian is in middle school and he argues with me because he'd rather play video games than do his homework. Now, I'm sure by the time Adrian is in middle school, video games will probably *be* homework, but it will be my job as his dad to say, "I don't care that you don't want to do your homework. Homework is good for you!" Someday, when he's an adult, he'll call me up and say, "Thank you, Dad—thank you for forcing me to do my science homework (or read a book or practice piano). I love you."

It's my job as Adrian's dad to help him become the person he's meant to become. To help him become the best version of himself. Part of how I do that is working every day to become the best version of myself. To show him that happiness, love, beauty and care for others are things we can *choose* to have, and that those things make us richer than any amount of money ever could. I believe that as a father, it is my duty to help my son go further.

It's okay to have doubt. To worry that you're doing it wrong. Doubt is actually an awareness that there is a version of you that has capabilities beyond what you dare to dream. There is a future version of yourself that has accomplished everything you've ever hoped for and more. When you have feelings of doubt, ask yourself, "Why?"

Maybe you are afraid that you really are stronger than you think—stronger than the rational mind will allow. You may carry fear of failure, but behind this fear is an underlying limiting belief. The belief is that you are undeserving or unworthy. But the truth of the matter is that you are *worthy.*

You are powerful, and you do have the strength to discover that power and to wield it with grace and honesty. It's a good thing to have doubt, not only because you acknowledge your humility, but also because a deeper part of you recognizes the tremendous power you hold within you.

My favorite definition of Hell is: when you die, you meet the version of you that you could have been. You meet that higher version of you that could have achieved everything you've ever wanted to achieve and you think, "Wow—there's a big gap between this me and the real me, and I wasted my life." I don't want that for myself, for my son or for *anyone.*

So how do you avoid that? How do you avoid becoming a has-been or a never-was in your own life? I don't have all the answers, but I think it goes a little something like this:

Imagine you're cleaning your garden. Your garden will never be done. Leaves will always fall down, and plants will always die, but at some point you say, "Okay, maybe I'll work in my garden for an hour." You work hard for the hour. You get sweaty and hot and tired. Your garden is cleaner than when you started, but it's not perfect. Then you take a break.

Maybe you soak in your hot tub and admire the work you've done. You count the roses and the avocado trees and think, "Man, how lucky am I to have this beautiful garden?" And then you think, "Man, how lucky am I to be soaking in this beautiful hot tub?"

The next day, you do it again—the gardening, the sweating, the soaking, the admiration. Instead of feeling like this is a burden—like it's a punishment to have to weed your garden every day—you think of it as a blessing. Because you're outside, the sun is shining, the air is fresh and with your own two hands and your own open heart, you're committed to building something beautiful and to loving something enough to devote yourself to its care.

To feel love flow from your heart into the world and, in turn, feel love flow back from the world into your heart, like a gentle wave crashing onto the sand before returning home to the vast ocean.

To tend the fire within your soul and then use it to change the world. To change *your* world.

That, quite simply, is what it means to burn-in.

———

The role of the gallbladder is to store bile produced by the liver in its liquid form. When your mouth eats fat, the gallbladder contracts to push that liquid into the intestine and break down fats for easy absorption.

It is all fine and dandy when things are going smoothly—when the bile is fluid and you're going with the flow. But if you are a gallbladder and you are stagnant, you get attached to the bile and rather than pushing it out, you hold on! You cling to the bile, and it sits, which creates little stones over time. The stones try to flow along with the liquid and pass

through the duct but instead end up blocking it, getting caught in the duct
and causing pain, inflammation, infection and even sometimes death.

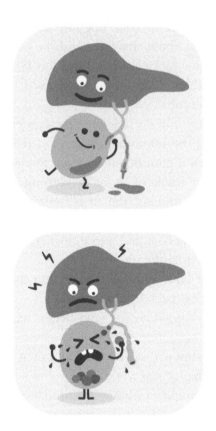

    Your conscious experience throughout life is one flowing river, one
stream progressing in one direction: forward. If you try to cling to past
experiences, to cling to a boulder or rock in the river path, to hold on to
trauma, hatred, bitterness, resentfulness, anger, anxiety, fear and a victim
mentality, then you will suffer these pains any time the stone gets in the
way of the natural flow of things.

Hold on to resentment, and it is bitter. It will harden into stone such that it blocks your path to happiness, the normal flow of your energy, causing you pain.

The key to finding bliss and joy in every moment is to let go. Even though it hurts, pass the stone. Let it go and allow the river to flow again.

Afterword

There is a different energy when you go from an inch deep and a mile wide to an inch wide and a mile deep. When maybe instead of having 5,000 Facebook friends, you have five true friends you can call on anytime, day or night. Maybe you read five books a year but read each one multiple times.

Maybe there's one chapter in this book that jumped off the page and grabbed you by the arms and shook you into thinking about something in your life in a totally new way.

Maybe there's another chapter that didn't click for you. That's okay! My greatest wish for you and for your relationship with this book is that it's a long and happy one, where you feel like you can come back to it and come back to me as your life changes, as your wants and needs change.

I hope that my wants and needs change, too. I hope I never stop changing, actually—that I'm able to see the beauty in change and growth. I'm not perfect and I never will be, and I feel at peace with that statement in part because there was a time when I didn't know if that was the kind of statement I could even make.

This is just the beginning for me, and I hope it's the beginning for you, too! I'm honored that you took the time to read what I have to say, and I'd love to continue this journey with you at wealthbound.com, where the conversation on real estate investing and what it can do for you is ongoing.

I'd also like to suggest some further reading that I've categorized using the pillars of WEALTH:

Wealth

Money: Master the Game by Tony Robbins
Misbehaving by Richard H. Thaler
Principles by Ray Dalio
Secrets of The Millionaire Mind by T. Harv Ecker
The Snowball by Alice Schroeder

Elevation

Vivid Vision by Cameron Herold
Untethered Soul by Michael Singer
Siddhartha by Herman Hesse
The Vortex by Esther and Jerry Hicks
How to Change Your Mind by Michael Pollan

Action and Accountability

Tiny Habits by BJ Fogg
Loving What Is by Byron Katie
The Checklist Manifesto by Atul Gawande
Liminal Thinking by Dave Gray
Success Affirmations by Jack Canfield

Love

Keys to the Kingdom by Alison Armstrong
The 5 Love Languages by Gary Chapman
His Needs, Her Needs by Willard F. Harley Jr.
Out of the Doghouse by Robert Weiss
The Alchemist by Paulo Coelho

Time

The 4-Hour Workweek by Tim Ferriss
The ONE Thing by Gary Keller
Blink by Malcolm Gladwell
Deep Work by Cal Newport
Who Not How by Dan Sullivan

Health

Be Here Now by Ram Dass
Opening the Door of Your Heart by Ajahn Brahm
The Power of Habit by Charles Duhigg
Essentialism by Greg McKeown
Karma: A Yogi's Guide to Crafting Your Destiny by Sadhguru

I also promised a TLDR for the nuggets I gave up front. As you are graduating from this book, I have just three goodies to go over:

Keep a Beginner's Mind

This means to think about things as if you're brand new, even if you've been doing it for 30 years. Or just always think about things in a new light. Yes, you need expertise and a framework to think deeply about things—but that's just the bare minimum. In medicine, I would say that it's like just passing the standard of care. But you'll never be a great physician by treating everyone like they're a case in a textbook. Patients and diseases do not read textbooks. There are rare presentations of common diseases and common presentations of rare diseases. So, learn it all and then go heal people.

Go beyond the protocols to see what will help that one person in front of you. A complication rate may be one percent, but if it happens to you or to your patient, it is 100 percent for you or that patient. In real estate, the highest volume flippers and the people I know who found success the fastest went out and hustled and crushed it. They flipped 50 houses a month because they didn't learn from somebody who said that they typically do 50 houses a year. So, the new guys, without the limits from dogma or from anybody else in the industry getting mediocre results, went out and succeeded because their mindset was free to explore doing things in a bigger way.

For a long time, people thought it was impossible to run a sub-four-minute mile. Then, as soon as one guy did it, everyone else started doing it like it was no big deal. That first guy broke the barrier for everyone else and changed the world's mindset. As a health-care professional, if you keep an open mind and a beginner's attitude, you may see something that doctors and nurses and administrators have seen for 30 years as a problem with no solution—and you might instantly come up with a solution.

Be Kind

Be kind to yourself first. I know all the negative things I've ever spoken to myself in my head, so I can only imagine what might be running through yours.

You want to know what it was like to be in my head before? *You're fat. You're short. You're too Asian. You're not Asian enough. You don't deserve to be here. Who said you could do that? What's wrong with you? Why can't you do anything right? You'll never be good enough. You're nothing. You're trash. You're scum. You deserve this horrible situation you're in. You're ugly. Nobody will ever love you. Maybe it'd be better if you were dead.*

And then do you know what I said to other people? Sometimes better, sometimes worse stuff.

You know what I used to do when someone would make a

little mistake when driving and they'd cut me off, not see me in the left lane or they were driving too slowly? I would gun it, flip them off, honk and brake check them before speeding off. I used to sigh loudly and complain that some lady in front of me had too many items in the grocery store. These things all came from my ego and my selfishness. When you realize that the guy or gal next to you actually *is* you, or at the very least is deeply connected to you whether you know them or not, then you'll be okay.

My son may have cancer, but your son may have been murdered. One is not better or worse than the other. It's not a competition. You don't compare problems. You share grief so that the load is lightened. You be a friend and show compassion to the stranger bawling on the floor because her child just died. You go help the girl in front of the bar in downtown Mountain View when she is too drunk and the idiots with her are trying to call her an Uber when she needs an ambulance, and you prevent her from getting raped or dying from alcohol poisoning that night.

You see a woman who is running away from an abusive man in the street, and you stop your car, take her somewhere safe and call the cops. You see a young woman, mouth bloodied, and waving down cars asking for help while running away from her abusive boyfriend and you stop your car, take her somewhere safe and call the cops. And in Texas, you can kick the guy's ass because you are acting as third-party self-defense, but in California you would get arrested for doing that. Texas may not have all of the best laws, but that's a good one for sure. I wish these were just examples from TV or movies, but these have all happened to me or people close to me.

The point is this: our time on this earth is limited. You and I and everyone we love will die one day. And it's a beautiful thing. I never thought about it before Adrian's diagnosis, but now I think about it a lot.

There are some cool series that I would suggest you check out on Netflix including one called *Surviving Death*. There are many books where people describe near death experiences (NDEs). I'm in many Facebook groups for physicians, and in one of them, an experienced emergency room doctor asked if anyone's patients ever told these stories. Following that, maybe 1,000 comments and reactions came up. This was my response to the skeptics and the believers alike:

I'll tell you what. Medicine and Western science cannot explain it all. Your consciousness or soul or whatever you want to call it does not go away when your physical form dies. Your rational mind and ego will tell you it's BS when the patients come back and they see white light or feel infinite peace before they are shocked back into rhythm and into their bodies again. Because there's no scientific method or theory or whatever to explain something on a plane we don't have the capacity to understand right now. In the meantime, though, their soul/Self/Atman/whatever you want to call it is liberated from the flesh and they can see it as it really is, if only for a moment.

When they are pseudo-dead, they're free from the body, which has physical pains. As a human, you still have to eat, drink, pee, poop. Your bones hurt as you age—my patients tell me every day that I shouldn't get old. I jokingly reply that it beats the alternative, but now that I think about it, I will stop saying that. Because it probably doesn't. There's no understanding the feeling of infinitely being a part of the universe unless you've experienced it yourself. Or meditated your way there. Or whatever your path was to this understanding.

At this point you should realize that while you may think you're hot shit and know it all as a doctor, the truth is you don't. You have a limited view of the world from your own

two eyes, however open you have them—and however open
your mind is, too. And nobody has all the answers. It is
when we put them all together and see it from every angle
simultaneously that we can truly see it. And that happens
when you die or leave your body or whatever.

When we understand this, when we stay humble and
recognize we don't know it all, then we can be better
doctors. And we can serve patients with unlimited
compassion. And we can heal ourselves and the whole
world.

Death is something not to be feared the way that most
do. How many patients are clinging to life on a vent with no
quality of life and how many docs and nurses and hospitals
are a party to this clinging to a dying physical form? I know
when I die, if I can choose to, I want to not be hanging on
to anything. I don't want anyone to guilt me into hanging
out for another hour so they can see me intubated and
sedated, and I can't get out of the bed to poop for myself.

Our time on earth is limited. Maybe it's 100 years,
maybe it's tomorrow. So don't waste time being upset and
burned out and a jerk to other people. I've been there: it's a
waste of the precious life we've been granted here. My son
is fighting for his life at two years old with a rare kidney
cancer called clear cell sarcoma of the kidney. Think Wilms
tumor, but more aggressive with a more aggressive
treatment in terms of adjuvant radiation and chemo. I think
about death a lot.

I also think about what it means to be a great doctor a
lot.

I'm super open to these ideas that the patients tell us
when they die and come back. It's like a sacred space they
enter, and they can share this knowledge with us that we
otherwise would not get a chance to learn about, unless we
die or almost die ourselves.

People came out of the woodwork after I posted this. Dr. Elizabeth Gnagy DO, a physician board certified in Psychiatry and Addiction Medicine, messaged me afterward, telling me that my comments helped her process the loss of her son.

During the first week of school in August 2016, 13-year-old Jacob Scott was walking to the bus stop when he was hit by a car; the driver had been blinded by the sunlight that day. Jacob's death was a tragic loss for his family and seems nonsensical to us as human beings; however, in death, he was able to serve others as an organ donor.

Jacob saved the lives of two other teenaged boys, a 13-year-old and 17-year-old, with his kidneys, as well as an adult with his liver and another adult with his heart. Yes, it is horrible that he lost his life, but we must also consider what an incredible gift of life to those other four beautiful human beings who also deserved to live!

When you zoom out of the situation, you can see that the loss of life is excruciatingly painful to Jacob's family while simultaneously bringing exponential gratitude and life to others with a leveraged impact. The loss of one life touches the lives of so many others with both sorrow and joy.

It is comments like these that tell me I am headed in the right direction. We all carry a little voice inside of us—it is called intuition. When we listen, we will be safe. And our inner light will guide the way.

Think Critically, For Yourself

When I was in medical school, I was taught to not inject lidocaine with epinephrine into acral sites like a digit, nasal tip, ear, penis and so on out of fear that the vasoconstriction would cause necrosis. This was echoed by my fellowship director in Mohs micrographic surgery. People still think this all the time and will use plain lidocaine, which is way worse because you don't get the hemostatic effect of epinephrine during surgery, you can't safely use as much medication because of lidocaine toxicity and now you're operating in a field where it pools with blood all the time.

Did you know that this fear is pure dogma, passed down from generation to generation of doctors with no real data behind it? In fact, the plastic surgeon Donald Lalonde performed pivotal studies that demonstrated the super clear safety of using lidocaine with epinephrine anywhere.

There are countless other examples in medicine. In every textbook you read for a melanocytic lesion, the answer to the question, "How should one sample this spot?" is excisional biopsy. I will tell you probably 99.9 percent of board-certified dermatologists will do a deep shave when they're concerned about malignant melanoma. Yes, I have heard horror stories of doctors who didn't know what they were doing harming patients by doing incomplete biopsies. These are not the people who should be biopsying! A board-certified dermatologist is for sure the one to shave your melanoma. Just don't do it yourself, and don't let an unqualified person do it. There doesn't need to be this insane rift between plastic surgeons and dermatologists with regard to this "controversy."

Another derm-related thing is Accutane (isotretinoin), the acne curing medicine, which was and is still thought by many to create poor wound healing. Surgeons and doctors in general are afraid to operate on someone who's recently finished Accutane. If you can find me a good study demonstrating this, then I will gladly wait six months to do anything for my patients who have just finished Accutane. Until then, I suspect that this, too, is dogma, based on some theoretical paper in the '70s with a hypothesis that istotretinoin inhibits the follicular units and thus inhibits wound healing. Prove me wrong. I'm waiting.

It has been my sincere pleasure presenting this to you. I hope you find this book worthy of re-reading, and we become friends.

Aho. Namaste. Peace be with you. Safe travels.

Patrick, Dr. Tran

GATE GATE PARAGATE PARASAMGATE BODHI SVAHA

Acknowledgments

Family: To my wife, Alicia, for teaching me that there is no limit to love and compassion. To my son, Adrian, for showing me the meaning of life, teaching me how to put others before myself and reminding me to find Grace through every challenge. To my Vietnamese refugee parents, Myngoc and Chi, for showing me the value of a strong work ethic and for financially, emotionally and spiritually supporting my extensive education. To my big Sea Star, Natalie, the Kindergarten teacher, for teaching me to break down complex concepts to explain as if to a five-year-old. To my little brudder Eric, the musician and pianist, who taught me to follow my dreams, and for listening to Mom to become a doctor, only not the kind she expected.

GoBundance: Matt O for getting me into GoBundance and JDC; Jason Drees for the key phrase; Brodie Whitney for coaching me through some of life's inevitable struggles; Darryl Putnam for his support as a fellow writer; Jake Harris for his endless ideas and connections; Derek Clifford for sharing many author resources with me; Tom Burns who blessed me with time and support as a fellow physician and author; Chong Foo, you're in the book, dude, check it out! Darren McMahon thanks so much bud for your advice and support! To Huy Le, for being a great role model not only as a fellow Vietnamese doctor who promotes physical fitness, but also an entrepreneur and chicken farmer—everyone that's not vegan, go eat more chicken! Thanks to the rest of the NorCal tribe, Aaron West, Joe Martin, Calvin Chin, Wilson Leung, Ryan Stenberg, John Lockwood, Chris Dunham, Larry Chan, Dale Corpus, Aaron Nelson, Tariel Gusseinov, Beau Eckstein, Tony Trinh, Cliff Tsang, David Greene and whoever else—don't cry if I didn't put your name up because I'm only human and I still love you.

Special shout out to Daniel Del Real—you are one of my best friends and I feel so grateful and honored to know you. Thanks for reading the manuscript in one fell swoop on your flight from Colorado to California and thanks for helping my family get into the house we deserve to live in. You're amazing and I cherish having you as a friend. To Brett Levine, for essentially adopting me into your family and helping out this younger doc—thanks for being a gracious host and allowing me to crash at your place while recording the audiobook.

Book Team: To Jaime Hope for your support as a fellow doc and introducing me to my publisher. Anna David and the entire crew for believing in me and prioritizing my story. Angela Serratore for her amazing writing—we're going to the moon! Kaitlin for project management. Thanks to Onur Aksoy for not the cover I wanted (at first!), but the cover I needed.

Also thanks to Amanda Zieba the Word Nerd for helping me take my first steps as a writer before this book and helping me execute my first book ever: *The Tran Hammer Method*, which is an intuitive way to solving the Rubik's Cube without memorizing a ton of algorithms.

SmartVA: Thanks to Kristi Yoder for creating an amazing company, to Karen Pusta my weekday EA, Mama Rica my weekend VA and Regine my accounts manager who helps me through you; Laurice for project management, Ann for indulging my social media post ideas, Joselle for logos, both Joshuas, Adrian Dy for having a cool name and doing my websites, Diane for bookkeeping and the whole army for allowing me to channel my passionate energy.

Meditation: To Dina, for teaching me to sit within myself and go deeper. To Dana Marin, for unlocking infinite joy during meditation circle. To Vika, for teaching me grounding techniques and for reminding me that the loving awareness I feel during retreats is something that I carry with me always in my heart. To Paul Makielski, for the realization that the ultimate version of me is a pure vessel of love. To Cyber Chuck, for being there for me when I felt so up in the air and for the phrase, "He gets it!"

CSI: Thanks to Greg Morganroth for the incredible surgical training and for being a mentor and role model in business. To Dr. Kristelle Lusby, for going to bat for me when I was still an integrated plastic surgery resident and you were my chief resident; also for telling me to come train at the place where I love to work now. To Dr. Rossitza Lazova, for your world class dermatopathology expertise, always answering my texts promptly and helping me write my upcoming textbook. To everyone at California Skin Institute, from management to back office to front office, thank you for the love you have shown me during a trying time for my family. To all my patients who have inspired me with love and shown me the value of time, peace and gratitude.

Kaiser: To Dr. Yamout, for getting Adrian's cancer out en bloc, keeping it stage II and not seeding tumor through the rest of his body and to Dr. Beleneski for being first assist. Thanks for your compassion and expert explanation which was helpful not only to myself as a surgeon but as a father and a patient. Our interaction has changed the way I practice medicine, and I will never take for granted the faith placed in me by my patients and their families when I do a big surgery like a forehead flap to reconstruct an entire nose that was lost to a nasty skin cancer.

To Dr. Jason Kelley, for explaining the rationale for radiating across the spine to avoid scoliosis, but at the cost of an inch or two of height. For Precious, for amazing care and coordination.

To the other Dr. Tran (Hung), Adrian's primary pediatric oncologist; to Dr. Laura Campbell for her encouragement of my charitable endeavors; to Caroline Hu, Maria Maruffi, Lisa Goodman, John Kim and the entire team at Kaiser Oakland for caring for my precious son. To APIC Jorge Guttierez for accepting my loving mother's many calls. To the residents, including Krista Roberts, good luck with the rest of your residency and thank you for validating my efforts—I hope this book helps you and many of your colleagues. Thank you, Marta Calvo, for coordinating Adrian's care so carefully. To the Children's Oncology Group, including Dr. Elizabeth Mullen, for your incredible research on renal tumors and caring for kiddos with rare diseases.

To all the incredible nurses, but especially Miss Dorothy, Miss Jean, Miss Charlene. Also to Hing for feeding us yummy treats. To Jean Quigley, who educated us at the beginning on the whole chemo plan and for demonstrating the injection of GCSF by literally stabbing yourself in the arm with a clean needle when you really didn't need to do that.

El resto: To all my instructors in life from extra-curricular to school, from kindergarten teachers at St. Leo's who sent me home with brown apples on the color scheme every day (for reference red is good, followed by green, then yellow, then my speciality) through the 25th grade. To all the people who ever gave me a hand and taught me something when they didn't have to.

To Drs. Adam Cohen and Bill Sando, for sharing your wisdom with me as plastic surgeons a bit ahead of me in life when I was just an intern.

To the random guy whose car I rear-ended on the freeway after slamming my brakes in the rain while driving from Indiana to Virginia when I was switching over from plastic surgery residency to dermatology and who didn't ask me my insurance, just made sure his trunk worked and went along his day—thank you for that. To all the cops who ever pulled me over for little things and didn't give me a ticket because I really wasn't hurting anyone. To the random-act-of-kindness stranger who put some quarters in the parking meter that I forgot to pay on a Saturday in Berkeley and saved me a $40 ticket from the meter maids.

In memory of Paul DeWolf, my medical school classmate, you are missed and loved. To his mother Kris, sister Rebekah and father Thom for their kind words and special review of my book.

To Chris and Danielle Davis, thanks for helping us with our home and hair during a tough time for my family. To Chris and Tony Sims, thanks for the beautiful new shower and for being flexible in supporting our family during this journey. To Bulmaro and Gio Marquez, for getting the pool from green to clean and keeping it that way. To Frank Natale, my fish guy and friend. To George Lee, for the beautiful ancient stone necklace and bracelets you crafted for me to match my high energy while grounding and protecting me. To all our neighbors who show us love by checking in on us and allowing Adrian to trespass on your property to talk to your trees and pick your flowers. To my many friends and family, too numerous to count, who were kind enough to read the manuscript, to inspire me, to support and love me during this incredible journey.

About the Author

Dr. Patrick Tran is one of the only dermatologic surgeons in the Central Valley of California with fellowship training in Mohs micrographic surgery.

He graduated summa cum laude from the University of California, Berkeley with a degree in Molecular and Cell Biology and has published articles in numerous peer-reviewed journals, including *JAMA Dermatology, Plastic and Reconstructive Surgery, Plastic Surgery* and *Journal of Dermatological Science*.

He has delivered presentations nationally at the American Academy of Dermatology and regionally at the Washington D.C. Dermatological Society and the California Society of Plastic Surgery.

His program for doctors looking to leverage their income, Wealthbound, launched in September 2021. *Burn-In* is his second book.